Manic Episodes and the Dark Side

Manic Episodes and the Dark Side

a Memoir of a Bipolar Life

Richard R. Patton

iUniverse, Inc.

Bloomington

Manic Episodes and the Dark Side
a Memoir of a Bipolar Life

iUniverse books may be ordered through booksellers or by contacting:

iUniverse
1663 Liberty Drive
Bloomington, IN 47403
www.iuniverse.com
1-800-Authors (1-800-288-4677)

ISBN: 978-1-4620-0461-4 (sc)
ISBN: 978-1-4620-0462-1 (ebk)

Printed in the United States of America

iUniverse rev. date: 03/17/2011

Acknowledgements

To my sister Pat, who never gave up on me, used all the resources available to her to get me out of trouble and secured the medical help I required. Without my sister and her love, I would have long since given over to living in a cardboard box, panhandling the intersections and convenience stores. It is to her I dedicate this book.

To my sister-in-law Lois, whose editing skills and constant encouragement made this book possible.

To my brother Ralph, who in many ways took the place of my father by providing tough love and confident, heated advice. Without his and Lois' reinforcement, this book would have remained a thought.

To my son-in-law, my best friend and confidant, who always exemplifies the Christian Brother.

To my children, for their love and forgiveness in the face of my lifelong selfishness and failure as a father.

To others on these pages whose names have been changed, but who have shared my life's journey.

Contents

Prologue

A true friend is one soul in two bodies.
Aristotle

It has been twenty-one years since his death and I still ache as I recall the joy and innocence with which he met his fate. He seemed to have recaptured the carefree spirit of his youth, yet moments later, it was taken away.

Even before it happened, I knew a great work was unfolding: God had willed him to die.

I'd had the same dark premonition many years ago when I was moved to prepare, in precise detail, a small apartment for my mother. I sensed she would die within hours of her happy homecoming. She did.

This time I felt the same certainty. None but the Almighty could have orchestrated the chain of events that had led to such an unlikely and abrupt tragedy. One split-second sooner or later would have made the incident merely a close call, something to thank God for.

Out of a quiescent predawn fog, the monster of death came forth with a singular purpose in mind. My kindred spirit seemed mesmerized—drawn toward the light emanating from the steel beast. After what seemed like an eternity, I decided to prove my faith. I didn't call out. The terrible collision of unforgiving iron and soft flesh made a crushing sound that pierced the early morning peace. Even now, I can relive each moment of the event.

Running to him, I removed and laid my crucifix on his trembling chest. Passion and regret surged from my breast where the charm had been dancing. He had been the source of nothing but warmth, love and joy since we met. All the pleasant experiences we had shared passed before my eyes. He had trusted me completely. Though I cherished him, I had let him down this once and God seemed to have taken his life.

It is at this point in a manic episode that I alternately experience waves of unspeakable joy and unending incredible horror, sometimes within the course of only a matter of minutes. Either God was with me, speaking to me, or He had deserted me entirely.

The appearance of crimson blood on the radiant pure gold cross gave rise to a hope inside. I prayed for a miracle. Surely, this tragic mistake could be reversed. Take him to the hospital, I told myself. I had wheels for speed.

I must have averaged better than 130 mph trying to rendezvous with an emergency physician in the city thirty miles away. While winding out fifth gear, I heard what sounded like a pebble hit a wheel well. I continued to drive like a maniac despite the increasing problems with loss of steering.

Arriving at my destination, I quickly checked out the car. I discovered that I had navigated on only three tires while clipping at least three other cars as I wove in and out of traffic. Those drivers and the police would surely understand the urgency of my mission, I thought. A small white sports car arrived with me on the scene. Out stepped a beautiful, Latin doctor wearing a white coat with a stethoscope around her neck. She followed me to the patient. I could not watch, I just stood by and tried to commune with God. In a few moments she gave me her prognosis. I cried. She held me. No procedure available to man would work.

Even a lethal injection to end the pain had become unnecessary. Where had God been? The only sentient being willing to have a close relationship with me was gone. God had taken everything. He had surely damned my soul. My dog was dead!

PART ONE: Early Years

1951-1973

One – Under the Piano

Music is the shorthand of emotion.
Leo Tolstoy

My earliest memory this side of the womb is of sitting under the baby grand piano next to the stairway in our living room. Nothing brought me more joy nor made me feel more secure than seeing my mother's high heels on those three pedals as she began to play. Even as a five-year old, I sensed her skill and passion for her repertoire of Renaissance, Baroque, Classical, and Romantic era pieces. The musty smell added to the ageless sound emanating from the huge soundboard. In the semi-darkness, I took in the music through my ears and felt it vibrate all through my body and soul.

Calm and gentle Jesse Lee of French-English ancestry submitted to my father when necessary, but skillfully "handled" him when it suited her. She was my confidant advocate and friend. My mother was gracious, pretty and charming—a proper lady.

My father, B.W. Patton—Mother called him Pat, as did most of his friends—was a sharp contrast to Mom. He was often dogmatic and contentious, but was a loving father in spite of his personality. (He was usually right, anyway.) I knew his given name was Bernard, but only after seeing his passport was I certain the W stood for Washington. He was named after his grandfather, Alexander Washington Patton.

Dad received his medical degree from the University of Tennessee, went into public health work and then served in WWII, running a M.A.S.H. unit in the Philippines. For most of my lifetime, he worked as a gastroenterologist at the V.A. hospital in St. Petersburg, Florida. After retiring, he took a position as ship's physician aboard Norwegian Cruise Line ships operating in and around the Caribbean islands and South America. He had worked with veterans for so long, family members had to remind him to soften his brusque bedside manner. Mom cruised along with him for several years before her death in 1977 at the age of sixty-three.

I was born May 31, 1951 in St. Petersburg, Florida. My siblings often reminded me of the years it took for Dad to talk my mother into having another child. He hoped for another son to carry on the family name. Mom had lost two babies at birth and was happy with the family she had. However, I became the son of my father's old age, and like Jacob's twelfth son, Benjamin from Biblical times, he loved me the most. At least he considered me special and had high hopes for me. They named me Richard Roderick Patton; I was called Roddy until my mid-twenties. Like most of my family, I arrived with red hair and eventually acquired their freckled complexions.

I have two brothers, Ralph and Currie, and one sister, Patty. They are sixteen, fourteen, and seven years my senior respectively. My brothers had mostly moved from home when I was young. Ralph graduated from University of Tampa after roughing it through the Army National Guard—obviously a character-builder, but was not to make a career of the military as did his younger brother, Currie. Ralph married Lois, and with his combative personality, determination, and will to succeed, he began the successful rise to a rewarding family and career with his equally resolute and achieving wife.

Currie joined the US Army a semester short of graduating from college but later finished his BS, Officer Candidate School and a Master of Education degree. He married Claudia. He served a year in Viet Nam and received the Purple Heart for injuries in combat. Currie then spent a year in Korea. Claudia lived with my family whenever Currie was overseas. Claudia and I became buddies—we made our own pizza, watched *Saturday*

4

Night at the Movies, and, generally kept each other company when the folks were out. After Currie's twenty years, he retired as a lieutenant colonel and began teaching high school ROTC.

Dad kept me informed about my brothers, citing their sterling character and successful lives, in an effort to influence me to follow their paths. But by the time I reached my teen years. I felt certain I would never measure up to them. The goal seemed unreachable.

Patty was close enough in years to be a friend in my younger years and a virtual savior in my late twenties, especially after my mother's death, and remains so to this very day. Patty played rough football with the boys in the neighborhood. She was a good student despite having to suffer under Dad's impatient attempts to teach her algebra. Patty would frequently take me with her on the bus downtown to attend the movies. She and her girlfriends would bribe me with candy bars so I would let them comb my hair like the latest celebrities, but mostly Elvis Presley.

Pat spent a semester at Long Island University but ultimately graduated with a BA in Chemistry from Florida State University. The summer after my sophomore year in high school, while Pat was a senior living in Tallahassee, I received a summer music scholarship to FSU as a high school student; I played the trumpet and French horn. During the weekdays, we studied music theory, composition, conducting and practiced our various instruments for the orchestra. Monday through Thursday, I lived in the dorm like a regular college student. On the weekend, I could stay with my sister in her off-campus apartment. In those days, the summer of '65, Pat was just another semi-wild, fun-loving college senior. We went to Chanellos for pizza; Pat and her friends made sure I had my fill of beer, although I was too young to approach any of the hot college coeds at that time.

We took trips on motorcycles. Her friends let me ride on the back, and at times even let me ride their bikes on my own. One afternoon Pat and I went to the local Honda dealer and were approved to test-drive a large Honda road bike. With Pat on the back, I wanted to show her how fast I could accelerate. At about seventy mph, after winding out third gear, I power downshifted instead of taking it into fourth gear. Pat almost flew over my head. I retained control of the bike, but as soon as we returned to the dealer my sister hotly remarked, "I don't know what possessed me to trust my life to my little brother—I must be crazy!"

We often went fishing with her guy friends, taking potted meat sandwiches, plenty of Busch beer, and cane poles with worms. From a small boat we fished for anything that would bite. Those were some great times: Wicked enough to keep me from getting bored and supervised enough to keep me from my normal level of misbehavior.

No son ever had a better mother, father or siblings to influence his family life. Nor did I lack any love and encouragement, in spite of my increasing childhood, and later teenage, delinquency. Dad loved me enough to use the belt expertly and frequently as I grew older, but gave up this type of punishment out of desperation.

Two – Cabin Zero

One of the things being in politics has taught me is that men are not a reasoned or reasonable sex.
Margaret Thatcher

With caring parents and the advantages of a secure home life, it is fair to ask what led me down the path of delinquency. Could it have been early childhood experiences? Some character flaw? A brain that craved stimulation and abhorred boredom? Perhaps early manifestations of my illness? These remain open questions, but to tell my story, I must recount the years leading up to my first manic episode.

At the age of six, I was already terrorizing the neighborhood, throwing rocks at cars, discharging my dad's firearms at street lights, stealing from the *7-Eleven*, and coercing the neighborhood girls to play doctor. I became an accomplished liar, but could never fool Mom, Dad or the police: I was usually caught.

So, for four summers from age seven to ten, my folks sent me to an all-boys summer camp for eight weeks each year. I'm certain it was for their sanity's sake. The camp lay deep in the wilds of a Central Florida hammock by a lake. The counselors ran it like a young men's military academy. Campers who appeared weak, or who otherwise antagonized fellow campers with their whining, elicited no compassion, only shame. They became targets for bullying.

Early on, I decided to join the bullies. This put me in a tough place: there was always a bigger bully. I was not excessively athletic, nor was I especially tall or muscular—just mean and determined to appear fearless. Planned activities were part of each day: Cabin cleanup and inspection, canoeing, archery, arts and crafts, swimming, water polo, rifle practice (closely supervised), and football. If a counselor observed two campers pushing, fighting, or even cursing at each other, we heard him say the dreaded words, "grudge match," as he wrote down our names

The schedule called for boxing every Wednesday, which continued until midnight. Most of the campers were required to select an opponent and fight for three minutes. We labeled whiners as sissies and booed them out of the ring when they faked their fights.

The grudge matches started about ten o'clock. During my first two years the opponents I was forced to fight were usually larger and faster. That made no difference to the ringmaster: We were to fight until one of us did not get up—so there was no faking it. A good, long fight, whether you won or lost, earned a notch on your respected, imaginary "bully patch." The unspoken rule dictated that your foe in battle would leave you alone from then on or even become a friend.

Other nocturnal activities were equally savage, especially "Indian and Settler." The director divided one-hundred campers into two groups made up of members from each of the eight age-segregated cabins. As a result, both teams had about an equal number of members from every age group.

With a flip of the coin, one team became the Indians, the other the Settlers. Each camper wore a strip of a torn white sheet tied around his head, representing his scalp. The Indians took off their shirts to distinguish them from the Settlers and then were sent to hide in the dark woods, swamps and water around the camp. Sweat covered me as I fought myriads of buzzing and biting insects. I tripped over tree limbs and became stuck in the mud and tangled in thorn bushes. The Settlers were sent to fight the Indians after fifteen minutes. We had no rules—just do whatever we could to steal each other's scalps. The man with the most would emerge victorious.

The whiners often took off their own scalps and gave them to the enemy to avoid a beating. I couldn't do that; what would my circle of friends say? I fought numerous times every year on different teams. Once I took seventeen scalps before being severely beaten by some Indian I never saw coming. He took my scalp and the seventeen I'd captured. I designated him the unknown Apache war chief. With my head held high, I could make the long walk out of the vine-tangled, swampy mess to join the long line of campers at the infirmary. I showed my wounds of battle—what the nurse diagnosed as a scorpion sting, multiple lacerations of face and hands, and a broken nose. They treated the sting with the Director's used chewing tobacco, the lacerations with band-aids and antibiotic ointment, and stuffed my nose on both sides with a several gauze pads.

I always believed the Indians had the advantage: they had time to adjust to the dark. The most successful ones hung from tree limbs prepared to pounce on the unsuspecting, almost sightless Settler. They could fight off any resistance and rip the scalp off—being sure to get the ones in the vanquished fighter's belt or pocket—and quickly flee. We also played a mean game of Capture the Flag. Game-related injuries were not quite as high. It wasn't as much fun either. Weekly cookouts on one of two Indian mounds included watermelon, hot dogs, marshmallows, and ghost stories passed down over some thirty years. I became blood brothers with a full-blood Seminole Indian counselor.

When asked to be a junior counselor for Cabin Zero during my third year at camp in the summer of '59—I was eight—I accepted, thinking it was an honor. Zero housed the youngest campers: five-and-six year-olds. The adult counselor of the cabin also served as the arts and crafts teacher. One night, after all the very young campers were asleep, he urged my participation as he molested me. Playfully, he convinced me to let him fondle my genitals as he kept saying, "Now doesn't that feel good?" First with his fingers, then with his mouth he "tickled" me and made me feel good in a way I had never experienced. Then it was my turn to repeat the process on him. Finally, he showed me how he could really feel good if he tried long enough on himself. Although prompted to try, I wasn't completely successful. I didn't tell anyone, but I did ask for and receive permission to return to Cabin Five the next day. I felt ashamed and knew what had happened was wrong, but secretly the discovery of my own sexuality excited me.

Sometime in the fall of 1960, I heard my dad discussing one of the neighborhood boys, who was a homosexual. "I could tolerate anything from my sons, but that," he said with disgust.

I immediately decided to prove myself a good and active heterosexual the rest of my life. In less than two months after returning from camp, I had successfully demonstrated my true nature, beginning with my young female neighborhood "patients."

As I grew into adulthood, I could never understand what the big deal was for the many people who experienced something similar. It wasn't a topic to be brought up in casual conversation, and I never looked back to the camp event feeling I was to blame. I just never really thought about it. Years later I realized from a dream sequence why it took so many years before I could show physical affection toward a man. It was not until I learned others found such experiences shameful and with a lasting effect on their lives, that I began sharing my episode with others—always on a one-to-one basis. By then I was thirty-five-years old and twenty-seven years had passed since the incident in Cabin Zero.

Three – We Were Conquerors

But for my faith in God, I should have been a raving maniac.
Mahatma Gandhi

One Saturday later that summer of '59, two other nine-year-old friends and I discovered a creek leading to Boca Ciega Bay hidden under a crooked line of trees and brush. A lifelong phobia developed as the result of a discovery trip up this creek.

We imagined ourselves to be conquistadors under Ponce de Leon, who had landed only a mile north of the creek in search of the Fountain of Youth (or so the historical sign declared). Once through the brush and into a small stream of water, we made our way inland through the mostly ankle-to-knee-deep creek. After about a hundred yards, we discovered the source. The water flowed from a cave covered by vegetation with only a few open spots revealing concrete. Although in reality it was a storm drain, we preferred to believe a neatly rounded cave was calling for exploration.

We went to my house and gathered matches, candles, water, and some minimal snacks. I knew no questions would be asked that I couldn't answer with a reasonable lie. When we returned to the mouth of the storm drain, we discovered it was really an entrance to a Mayan temple in the jungles of Central America—we had no idea what we would find inside where darkness called. I entered first to maintain my reputation for being the first to try anything—a trait that remained with me for many years.

My friends followed. The water level was only three inches deep, making walking easier than it was in the creek. One-hundred and fifty yards into the darkness, we could no longer see the light from the cave's entrance. About forty-five minutes further on, the circumference of the pipe became smaller, so we had to bend over to keep going. With no fear, I led on and my company followed, quietly mumbling concerns I ignored. We stopped to put our names on the wall using the soot of the candles; we were conquerors. Another slower-going hour inward, we saw a dim light ahead. It gradually became brighter as we trudged along.

All at once we heard the sound of rushing water ahead of us, accompanied by slowly rising water. By the time it reached our knees, we were frantically discussing our options. Could we float on the water the two hours back to the creek? Should we push through the rising water to the light that now seemed closer? We were conquerors—always advancing. We pushed ahead harder. When we reached the source of the light we had only two feet of ceiling left above us and the water was still rising.

Here we found another four-foot pipe intersecting the cave pipe vertically. The light blinded us as we pulled ourselves up onto a one-foot-wide lip that circled the base of the perpendicular pipe. I looked up to let my eyes adjust and could see a manhole cover with the bright light shining through the few holes. Now the water had risen to fill the lower pipe and reached up to the lip.

I crouched to prepare to push open the manhole cover. It took all my strength to push it up a few inches. Oh, my God! The walls were crawling with roaches and Palmetto bugs an inch thick, packed all over themselves as they, too, were escaping the water. The instant I realized what I was seeing, hundreds, if not thousands of roaches took flight and began pouncing all over me—on my face, on and in my shirt, and up my pant legs. In seconds, panic provided the adrenalin for me to push up the manhole cover and hoist myself out. The roaches were dropping off in swarms; I ripped off my shirt, dropped my pants and beat my head and body frantically. When my horror subsided to a fast beating in my chest and my emotions simmered down, I found I was standing almost nude in the middle of four-lane 5th Avenue, to the shock of motorists who had stopped to avoid me and wonder what manner of evil this was.

Since I had opened the manhole and most of the roaches came up with me, my friends made it out with less trouble. The police told us the near-by Olympic-sized swimming pool at Admiral Farragut Academy was being drained for repairs, which accounted for the flood in the pipe. We were successful in our pleas to the cops to not take us home to our parents.

To this day, roaches terrify me. Snakes, spiders, rats, no problem, but when I see a roach, my first impulse is to reach for a large firearm.

I have always had an abnormal attraction to fire and very early found ways to explore my fascination. Vast areas of waterfront properties in Florida were created by dredging the bottoms of bays and waterways to pile up sand and form fingers of land that were then lined with seawalls. Before the filled areas could be developed, the sand had to settle for ten years. In a few years tall grass and small shrubs grew to cover the fill.

Many of these fingers were islands designed to be eventually connected by small bridges. In the winter, the grass turned dry, providing the perfect opportunity to set large fires—once we crossed the water in a small johnboat. The fires we set were long, narrow and downwind. They flamed up high, but quickly died out as they spread to another patch of dried grass. At various points, we could run and jump right through the high flames without suffering more than singed eyebrows. The flames, of course, burned themselves out when they reached a seawall.

In the garage loft at home, I discovered a lot of WWII ammunition Dad had apparently kept as souvenirs. Among these were bored out artillery shells, and hundreds of live .30 caliber rifle rounds, also used in machine guns. We could be soldiers.

I grabbed fifty of the live rounds and a small can of gasoline. Bobby, Ricky, Joe and I got on our bikes and headed for the battleground—the brush-covered fills. First, we built a substantial fire with driftwood and the fifty rifle rounds and covered it with gasoline. Next, we set a larger fire circling fifty-feet around us. All was ready, so we tossed a match into the driftwood and hit the ground running to a spot twenty-five feet from the live rounds. It took about as long as it would for corn to pop before the explosions began. I was wearing the red and black Nazi armband I had stolen from Hitler's arm at the Madam Toussaint's Wax Museum months before, so I felt invincible.

There was nothing for the casings and projectiles to hit (their range was insufficient to reach either Pasadena or St. Pete Beach—a half to three-quarter mile down range in all directions.) We waited to make sure the last popcorn had popped before standing up. I think three remained after we stood the first time, so we dropped and stood several more times. No one was hurt, at least not among my men. Rick said he was sure he had felt a whiz pass by his ear. We had won the battle against the Germans.

Spencer, a buddy of mine, took my suggestion and devised a way to simulate a napalm explosion. In the vacant lot behind our house, using a couple of bricks and a one-by-six board, about five feet long, we made a seesaw apparatus to launch the napalm. Our plan was to place a large coffee can filled with gasoline on the downside. Tossing a lit match into the can would only cause a small fire on the surface of the gas. The neat part was to stomp on the opposite end of the wooden board and witness a half-gallon of gas explode into a huge airborne fireball.

I was first, as usual. The heat generated was tremendous but tolerable for the short duration of the explosion. Spencer felt safe to repeat the process. He also met with success. We were not yet bored of the experiment so I was next to repeat it. My second time met with disaster.

The board slipped and rotated when I stomped on it. The fireball headed for the right side of my body. I raised my arms to cover my face, but my side and back became covered in flame. As I ran, I could hear the flames beating on me. Out of either instinct or dumb luck, I made it across the street to the sprinkler watering a sandspur-filled lawn. I rolled in the wet yard until I could no longer hear flames. Fortunately, I had not been wearing a shirt. When I got up, probably in shock, I said to Spencer, "Wasn't that cool?"

He replied with fear in his voice, "Your back and side are black and bleeding; I'll go get your mom."

"No, don't tell her." My back really hurt and the smell was terrible. I went in the house; Mom was upstairs. I climbed the bookshelf next to the fireplace to sit on the mantel below the wall air conditioner. The cold air gave some relief, but the pain grew worse. I gave in and let Spence get Mom.

She called our next-door neighbor to help us. Mom and I got in the back seat of Katherine's car, stopped quickly for some spray Unguentine for burns, and rushed to the ER at Mound Park Hospital seven miles away. I kept my back to the open window; the breeze gave some relief. Every time Katherine stopped for a light, the unbearable pain returned. Mom sprayed more Unguentine on my burns.

When I reached the ER, the attending physician immediately gave me an injection of morphine. I had almost lost my mind with the pain before the medication took effect. Once it did, I could watch the process for treating dirty third-degree burns: Phisohex soap in crushed ice administered with softly touching hands.

After eight weeks of bandage changes, putting up with the nasty smell, and holding my right arm out sideways, I counted myself lucky. Somewhat of a miracle, according to the physician, the only lasting damage would be the strange disappearance of all my freckles in the entire affected area. I developed a true respect for fire, though my fascination remains.

Four – Best Friends

Insanity in individuals is something rare – but in groups,
parties, nations and epochs, it is the rule.
Friedrich Nietzsche

I lived two lives in my junior-high and high school years. One life my family knew about, the other they did not. This second life centered on *the group*—seven of us who did most anything and everything together until the middle of my sixteenth year. By that time, I had thirteen arrests on my juvenile record.

Joe, a skinny bleach-blonde surfer-type was the druggie who started with huffing glue, paint and most anything else with a poison warning label. Later on, he supplied us with pot, acid, speed and PCP. (If you remember the 60s, you were not there.) I had enough sense to avoid the glue and paint scene. I tried everything else at least once.

The police had ceased simply taking me home to my parents. Joe and I were walking down 9th Avenue near 66th Street, lighting and throwing firecrackers as we went. I am sure the cop would have let us go with a warning and confiscated our combustibles had we not tried to lie our way out. Instead, we went to jail, the first time for both of us—but not the last.

Paul, a cocky brute with a defiant snarling smile, was a natural born criminal. The first time I brought him to my house my Mom admonished me, "I don't know why, but I think that boy is no good. I just don't like him—you shouldn't run around with him."

Waiting in the left turn lane at the busiest intersection in St. Pete, Paul noticed the liquor truck waiting in front of us had the padlock loose on the back doors. With no hesitation or explanation, he jumped from the front seat of Jeff's car, grabbed from the truck the first case of booze he came to, and jumped back in the car. Jeff nearly killed us all as he tried to get the three of us away, cursing the whole time. Paul had stolen a case of cheap King James Scotch. With the help of friends, we finished the case that night. We each had his own bottle, but none of us finished drinking it before puking his guts out.

I had learned vomiting was a good thing six months before. While being taken to jail for public drunkenness and disorderly conduct at a teen dance club, the kid in the back seat with me died right before my eyes from too much alcohol. I figured he forgot to puke.

The bad night with the cheap scotch precipitated a 5:00 a.m. search for a 7-Eleven where the donut vendors often left their products on the top of the phone booths (the stores opened at seven in those days.) Next we toured the neighborhood to find where the ice-cold milk had already been delivered to the boxes set outside back doors.

Before we discovered we could buy liquor at a package store on the beach in Pass-a-Grill, we learned how easy it was to put a pint of Italian Swiss Colony muscatel down the front of our pants. That remained our standby plan when we couldn't make it to the beach.

One afternoon I received a phone call from Paul (we were both fifteen at the time.) He was extremely excited and speaking very fast, "Hey, I got $250,000, I'm at the airport in Tampa, and I'll wait for you…. We can fly to Paris or something."

"Right Paul," I answered. He exaggerated from time to time. "Call Jeff you meathead." Anything, just to get him off the phone.

The next morning Jeff, a tall, skinny, easy-going member of the group, came to the house unannounced and whispered excitedly for me to come outside. He was holding a copy of the local newspaper. The headline read, "Youth Arrested at Tampa Airport in Extortion Plot." The article mentioned the extortion of a large sum of money. Paul had learned that Susan, a classmate and an only daughter, had lied to her wealthy parents about her plans and had actually gone off for the weekend with her boyfriend. Paul took advantage of the situation and came up with a scheme: He demanded money from her father and threatened to kill Susan if her father did not come up with the money or if he involved the police. Paul's plan almost worked; he collected the money from a drop in a Good Will box, under which he had dug a tunnel for the pickup. A taxi waited two blocks across the railroad tracks for his escape, but the police apprehended him at the airport when he attempted to secure a plane ticket. That was his third arrest as a juvenile; they put him in prison until he reached eighteen.

Marty, a cool self-confident character a year older than I, was my closest friend. I rode on the back of his motor scooter until I received my own when I turned thirteen. (Later, both Marty and Jeff had cars before I could drive.)

Marty and I were dating two sisters who lived just off Park Street. The guy who lived next door to them seemed to us to be an arrogant fool. One day he came home in his '57 Chevy with brand new Firestone Wide Ovals and Keystone Mag wheels. Marty and I were really irritated by his strutting around, so we devised a scheme to humble him a bit.

We came back about 2:00 a.m., quietly placed his car on cinder blocks and took all four tires and wheels. Our intention was to toss them back in his front yard— after giving him a week to worry. We hid the tires under my back porch in the meantime. I assured Marty no one could prove a thing and told him to just keep his mouth shut.

By this time the police knew both of us well. They went to Marty's school first, knowing he would be the easier mark, and told him that I had already blamed him for the crime. Confronted with my bogus accusation, Marty blurted out, "He stole them, they're under *his* back porch."

When they came to my school, they said nothing but "You're under arrest for grand theft." They turned me around and cuffed me for the trip to my back porch. Did the police believe we intended to return the wheels—that it was all a joke? Not a chance. This grand theft charge just became another item to add to my already lengthy arrest record.

Of the seven members of the group, Jeff and I were the only ones who escaped that way of life—Jeff by the time he was twenty years old and I when I was sixteen. Paul was repeatedly imprisoned for extortion, selling drugs and weapons, and is now serving a life sentence. Marty is also in prison for life, but as a high profile drug dealer from the mid-70s.

Joe has been in a nursing home for the past twenty-two years in a complete catatonic state. Tom, a quiet, would-be tough guy, committed suicide after his third try. I think he was twenty-five at the time.

Ruthie, the only girl in our tight group, was a cute tomboy-type who loved our sexual harassment and was a real fun gal. She died from an overdose while shooting heroin—just after her eighteenth birthday.

Five – The Fish House

Life must be understood backwards; but... it must be lived forward.
Soren Kierkegaard

I was suspended from school in seventh grade at numerous times for various infractions: bringing some of Dad's bourbon in a mayonnaise jar to a school dance, smoking, back-talking teachers, and vandalizing the hallways of our new school building.

The Fish House became my punishment for the suspension. Dad was not going to let me sit around the house for three, five, or ten days, much less go out with my friends. Dad's friend and neighbor owned frozen fish freezer warehouses downtown and a large fish processing operation on Pass-a-Grille Beach, which was run by another of Dad's friends.

Mostly black Raiford State Prison parolees—muscular and menacing—operated the processing plant. I arose in the dark to get to the plant by 6:00 a.m. and left by 4:00 p.m. if all the day's processing was completed. I was told to start the job of emptying a semi-truck of fish in wooden cartons stuffed with ice—the task everyone in the plant hoped to avoid.

It took all the strength and stamina I had to move, or hook-drag, the 60,000 pound load from top to bottom and front to rear of the truck—and then the mere five yards from the truck to the start of the conveyor belt where I dumped the smelly mackerel. I was not going to be a whiner among these guys, so I completed the chore without complaint. Three days on the job then back to school with l'eau de cologne de poisson, a long-lasting new scent I "knew" the girls would love. Right. The next time on the job, I learned to fillet the fish—physically easy, but boring.

Dad had said it time and again, but now remained silent as he drove me to the fish house and dropped me off. He knew I could read his mind. Dad's mind said, "If you keep it up Bud, you're going to end up like those prisoners, getting drunk all weekend, smelling like fish for the rest of your life and making forty-five dollars a week."

After only a few weeks in eighth grade, I was expelled. The principal told my mother in my presence, "This boy will never amount to anything." That really infuriated Mom. (Neither she nor Dad ever gave up on me completely.)

Parenthetically, this same man had to appear in my office twenty years later in a subservient role. He remembered nothing of the unpleasant incident, so I helped him recall my mom and politely rebuked him for having spoken to a parent in that manner. Mom was already gone by then; so she could not appreciate the irony.

Having been expelled, I could not attend a public school in Pinellas County, so my folks sent me away to a military school for the 1964-65 year— some two-hundred miles away. I could not receive visitors for three months—worse than being at summer camp.

The military school was far from being West Point. Most of the kids, grades seven through twelve, were sent there for the same reason I was— discipline. These kids had ranks, I did not—I was a private. I anticipated having a real problem with authority there. The cadets understood this definition of hazing: "to persecute or torture somebody in a subordinate position, especially a first-year military academy cadet or a fraternity pledge." I decided to treat the many student-based hazing encounters with the old grudge match concept from summer camp: instant-grudge match, through-the-drywall grudge match, brick-in-the-head grudge match, knuckles-when-you-least-expect-it grudge match. I beat up many of my superiors for which I received demerits. I stood at attention for what seemed like forever, did countless push-ups, was assigned extra work duties, and withstood disciplinary whacks. I never understood why shirts and pants had to be starched—they made me itch—or why I had to make my bed; I was only going to get back in it in a few hours anyway. I abhorred the place.

The Colonel told my parents at the end of the year that I was an extreme case and I would not be allowed to return the next year. But I made it through eighth grade without any suspensions, except the one that got me there in the first place. The military school did not suspend or send anyone home. It was more than capable of disciplining in its own way, in my opinion.

The Pinellas County School Board would still not allow me to return to the public school system. I was sent to Bishop Barry High School instead, an all-male Roman Catholic school. I attended the 1965-66 school year as a freshman.

I had two personalities—one for each life I was living. When associating with my group, I was fearless—constantly trying to maintain my wild and tough image. Unknown to my group, other times I participated in, and even enjoyed, activities attributed to "good boys." I went to church, sang in the choir with my folks, played in the high school band and orchestra, and sang in the school choir. I attended Sunday school from the time I was five until the end of grade six.

I understood there to be a somewhat antagonistic relationship between the Roman Catholics and the Protestants—Methodists in my case. To my young mind, the Catholics were idol worshippers, prayed to Mary, had a pope who claimed he was the very Word of God on earth, and conducted the Crusades, Inquisition and so on. Much later, I studied the Roman faith and the Reformation in great detail from the perspective of an adult. But while enrolled at Bishop Barry, I reckoned I was in the spiritual stronghold of the heretics.

This attitude permeated my thoughts and behavior. This time I could fight against the enemy with impunity, or so I thought. Suffice it to say, I severely tested the patience of the men in black and made a mockery of their rituals and faith. I received the appropriate disciplinary actions from the priests. I escaped being burned at the stake.

As had been the case in the military school, the Monsignor would not allow me to return for the next year. The summer that followed was a wild one: The group got together on a regular basis.

After a lengthy hearing in downtown St. Petersburg, the Pinellas County Public Schools finally decided to give me another chance. I entered Boca Ciega High School to begin the tenth grade in the fall of '66. (Several more suspensions took place throughout both my sophomore and junior year. Each time I would go back to the Fish House.)

The repeated involvement with the police during non-school hours forced my probation counselor to prohibit me from leaving the yard during the summer of '67 unless accompanied by an adult. My dad believed the axiom "Idle hands are the Devil's workshop," so he arranged a long project for me to undertake for the summer.

A friend of Dad's, whom I called Dr. Brown, had extensive experience building fiberglass boats. He was old as dirt so he usually sat back and directed, explained and just talked to me. We went together to Irwin Yachts on St. Pete Beach and found a discarded set of molds for an International 14 Racing Sloop. Irwin had discontinued production of this boat and the molds were in drastic need of repair before we could begin building—the wooden frames had rotted, but the fiberglass molds were still usable.

An accomplished teacher, Dr. Brown told me how to reframe the molds and after a few weeks we were able to begin building the boat itself. It is an interesting process, building a fiberglass boat. You actually paint the boat before you build it. In two months or so, we were ready for the maiden voyage.

I had learned to sail in tiny ten-foot long prams when I was ten. Reading Robert Manry's account, *Tinkerbelle: The Story of the Smallest Boat Ever to Cross the Atlantic Nonstop*, a tale about a thirteen- foot sailboat, piqued my imagination and instilled a love for sailing that has stayed with me all my life

The maiden voyage in the newly built boat gave me great satisfaction, but I think that as Mom and Dad watched from shore it also renewed their hope for their wayward son.

Six – Runaway

By all means, marry. If you get a good wife, you'll become
happy; if you get a bad one, you'll become a Philosopher.
Socrates

M y group had its own table in the cafeteria at school. Seldom did
anyone approach us: We were trouble, shunned by the whiners,
academics and good kids. This pleased us.

When a cute, petite girl in a pink dress that looked like it came off a
Barbie Doll came up to me and called me by name, I was stunned—then
embarrassed—when she said, "You need to come with me and Charlie to
church and meet Jesus."

Oh God, I thought irreverently. Then I gave an appropriate answer.
"Yeah, right."

Helen was in the school band, which is how we later came to know
each other. Within a month we developed a relationship that consisted of
our dating only in the daytime so I wouldn't have to meet her extremely
religious and strict parents. At night, she dated Charlie, who years later
became a Baptist preacher with five children. I dated other girls at night.

I am convinced Helen was drawn to the evil in me as a way to rebel
against her parents. Soon Charlie exited the scene. Mom had taught me
proper etiquette: I knew how adults should be treated and I also had a
somewhat religious background of my own. So I dressed up, combed my

hair back, and proceeded to impress her mom and dad with my manners and "good boy" nature. Helen and I began dating at night. I missed the easy sex of my former nightlife, but it took six months for me to have my way. The following month Helen told me she was pregnant.

With the ever-present pint of Jim Beam in my back pocket and always with a snoot-full, I was easily persuaded to run away and get married. We were both only sixteen, but just as our fellow students thought, we believed we could get married in Georgia.

Helen found a hundred dollar bill in her mom's Bible and I borrowed three hundred dollars from a friend who took my boat as collateral. Previously, I'd had use of one of my parents' cars. Now I needed one of my own. I paid another friend fifty dollars for his seventeen-year-old 1950 Ford. I made a run to the Pass-a-Grille package store to stock up on courage, packed a small beach bag with a few items, and went to pick up Helen while her folks were at work. It took us forty-five minutes to load the trunk and back seat with virtually everything Helen owned—she thought she'd never return.

She left a note for her parents. I figured my folks wouldn't really start worrying for a few days. I didn't know what to say anyway.

Folkston, Georgia was about two-hundred-fifty miles north, just across the state line. Taking Interstate 4, we left St. Petersburg at 11:30 a.m. It was early March of 1968.

I had driven the Interstate a few times in a late model car. The speed limit was seventy, but the old flat-head six-cylinder Ford was not built for my speed of seventy-five and eighty. Fifty miles up I-4, I heard a ticking, then a thump, and finally an explosion. The hood blew up in flames, but the smoke and fire did not last long after I pulled over. We were in the middle of nowhere. As I recall, a passing motorist was kind enough to stop and promised to notify a tow truck at the next exit.

The only service man, at the only gas station, at the only exit for many miles, examined the car and said, "You've thrown a rod. There's no way it can be repaired."

"Where can I buy another car?" I asked. The man pointed to the only other establishment at this exit—a junkyard. With my keen bargaining skills, I asked the junkman if he had a car he could sell me for a hundred-fifty dollars or under.

He had two cars. Both were on sale today for one hundred- fifty dollars. The old Nash Rambler looked like, well, an old Nash Rambler, so I choose the 1959 Pontiac; it had a radio. Our test drive was short, as was the transfer of all the stuff we were carrying.

We were back on the road with less than an hour lost, enjoying the radio and fresh breeze circulating about us. An hour later, when we exited onto a two-lane road north, the weather turned cold and rainy. As we hurried to roll up the windows, we discovered all four were missing—they were probably on another '59 Pontiac, whose passengers were warm and dry.

About dusk, when we pulled into a tiny, cheap motel in Folkston just across the Georgia state line, a steep driveway yanked the muffler and tailpipe assembly from the bottom of the car. The Pontiac had a 455c.i. engine, so as we drove up to the office we sounded like a Mac truck—a noise we became used to on the remainder of the trip.

The next morning we walked the two blocks to the ancient county courthouse. We had every confidence we would be married within the hour. And then the clerk told us, "Your parents must sign for you." Undaunted, we continued toward South Carolina, hoping we could be married there.

An hour later, driving through the middle of the Okefenokee Swamp, I heard a loud thumping above the roar of the engine. I immediately pulled over, hoping to avoid another explosion.

When I looked under the hood, I didn't find any excessive heat or smoke. Walking around the car, I saw the retread had split away from a tire. When I realized what the situation would be had this engine blown like the other one, I came to my senses and had an idea.

I knew my sister's in-laws very well. They lived in Jacksonville, but a little more than two months before they had been in St. Pete for New Year's Eve, attending a party at my parent's house. When I had learned they were staying at the Sheraton near the Skyway, I decided Helen and I could enjoy New Year's Eve in the privacy of their room while they enjoyed the party.

I approached the front desk, presented myself as the son, and received the key to their second story room. Within thirty minutes, we heard keys rattling at the door, and then murmurings. The chain on the door bought us time to get dressed. I pulled Helen to the balcony that hovered over some nice grass. I had made jumps further than that, but it was a no-go for my date. I opened the door expecting the worst.

The couple entered and with enthusiasm called out, "Hey ya'll, Happy New Year, ya want a drink?"

That New Year's Eve reception convinced me they would accept us now and give us asylum. So I turned the car south and we headed for these folks in Jacksonville once again.

They had once shown me where they hid the key, so when they didn't answer the doorbell, we let ourselves in. They returned a few days later and we learned they had been visiting my sister Patty and her husband at my house in St. Pete. They greeted Helen and me in their typical nonchalant fashion—as if they had expected us to be there.

"Did my parents say anything about us?" I asked.

"No, we asked about you but they just said 'same old stuff'," Doc answered.

We explained the situation. Doc, who was an M.D., asked Helen if she really *was* pregnant. She assured him she was, so he rose from his chair and went into his study. When he emerged a few minutes later, he showed us a note on his letterhead stating he had examined Helen and determined she was, in fact, with child. He gave me the letter and told us to drive back the fifty miles to Folkston and show it to the clerk.

The hundred-mile round trip netted a big zero; as sixteen-year-olds, we still needed parental permission.

When we returned to Jacksonville, Doc asked if he could call my dad. I could sense the fear in Helen. She dreaded the prospect of having to face her parents, but I told him to make the call.

"Tell him to come home; we will figure things out together," Dad said.

Her parents had apparently contacted mine immediately after reading Helen's note—it had mentioned she was pregnant. They promptly gathered at my house—our parents had never met each other. After a lengthy talk with my folks, they gleaned I was a certified juvenile delinquent, called the State Police, and had them start a search for a gray 1950 Ford.

Helen had met my parents on several occasions. I suspected Mom and Dad thought very highly of her—comparatively—and wanted to bless our union for the sake of their son. That is what Dad meant by "figuring things out." My father was an extremely wise man.

When we arrived at my house, my mom came out to meet us and immediately welcomed Helen with a hug and assurance that all would be well. Dad stood on the front porch smiling. Patty and Bob were living there at the time and they welcomed Helen as well.

After dinner, my family all went upstairs so Helen and I could have a private meeting with Helen's parents. Helen was in tears and very upset. We had already taken all her stuff up to my bedroom; she did not want to go home with her parents.

Her mother spent at least two hours asking questions to drive home the certainty of our sin. She scolded us severely over and over again. Finally she determined the next step was to find out for sure if Helen was pregnant. Dad agreed to refer Helen to an OB/Gyn friend of his. If the pregnancy was confirmed, we were to have a church wedding as soon as possible.

Her father never said a word until they were on the way out with Helen and all her belongings. Not speaking to anyone in particular, he angrily declared in the presence of all of us, including my parents, "I know it takes two, but I could just kill him!"

The next morning Dad and I picked up Helen and took her to the doctor's office. When Helen came out, she was wearing an ear-to-ear smile. We were to wed; she would be out of her parent's house for good.

Before we left the lobby, Dad offered the abortion alternative. This was illegal at the time, but he assured us it would be safe. He had a friend who was a practicing physician in another country. Neither Helen nor I had considered it, but we were both quick to dismiss the idea. Sheepishly Dad replied, "Just giving you the option, it's going to be tough for you kids."

Helen's mother decided to arrange the wedding the next week, hoping people wouldn't notice a baby would arrive after only six months. The others of us involved couldn't have cared less.

We had a small wedding in the garden of the same church that had hosted the nuptials for all three of my siblings. Sally, a mutual girlfriend, stood up with Helen, and my brother-in-law, served as my best man. It was a real church wedding with both Helen's pastor and mine, Dr. Hamilton, officiating. My probation counselor was there to remind me that I was technically now an adult and would be tried accordingly should I get into any more trouble.

A nice dinner at the Bath Club on Madeira Beach followed. Helen had already moved back into my bedroom but we had been kept apart until that night—our honeymoon. The next morning, I was up at five a.m. getting ready to go to work at the Fish House—my dad's character builder.

Since we could no longer attend our high school—the rules prohibited married students—we enrolled in night school a few days later. I searched the newspaper ads for job opportunities and made inquiries in the late afternoons.

Seven – New Life

You're freaked out that you're going to be having a child, and once you're looking after your daughter, it's the most beautiful thing in the world.
Ben Stiller

A concerned sixth-grade teacher five years before had referred me to a psychologist for testing. The results proved to my parents and me that I was a bored, but bright child who needed motivation. My IQ tested astonishingly high: I had no excuse. For the remainder of that school year I was challenged by Mrs. Gasner and made straight As—she was a genuine teacher. As evidenced by my grades and behavior, I must have become retarded and bored again when I moved into junior high. I remained that way until confronted with the challenge of night school and the need for work that did not involve fish. My desire for sufficient education to qualify me for a good job became an obsession.

Fish House in the day and school at night was a heavy weight. Night school seemed a joke: American Government, for example, consisted of reading a twelve-chapter text and reporting for testing when ready. I read the book in a week, took a multiple-choice test, and passed the year with a B. I handled the other courses in the same manner.

I had taken a semester of Geometry at Boca Ciega before entering Dixie Hollins night school. My grades in all other courses that year were Ds and Fs because of either multiple suspensions or my just not producing.

In Geometry, however, according to my teacher, Ms. Guise, I earned strait As before deducting 3 per cent per day for each day of my suspensions. So I decided to take the night school Geometry test without studying. Locked alone in a room in the office complex, I took the three-hour test. This one was not multiple-choice. I knocked on the door to signal I had finished and waited as the teacher graded the test—I had made a C.

When it came time for Helen to get a math credit I suggested she take Geometry. I promised I would teach her as she went through the class. Within a few weeks it became apparent that she had no aptitude for arithmetic, much less Geometry.

I told her to tell the teacher she was ready to take the test. The plan was for me to knock on the window of the testing room, get the test and take it for her. When I was sure she was alone I made my move: I took the test from her, went to the car, and under the dome light began working with protractor, compass, and ruler at hand. It was not the same test, so I worked vigorously but carefully.

After two-and-a-half hours, I returned the completed test to Helen. I went to the classroom acting as calmly as I could. Helen and the teacher were just leaving the room when the teacher looked at me and said, "You should be ashamed of yourself, Mr. Patton." I froze. She continued, "Your wife made a B and you made a C." Swallowing my pride, I turned to Helen and simply replied, "That's great, sweetie."

Within three months, I earned all the credits I needed for a diploma. However, I could not receive it until my normal graduation date, a year-and-a-half later. The night school principal gave me a letter to prove I had successfully completed the requirements for graduation. This would allow me to enter college.

Helen decided to wait on further education, since I would no longer be going with her to class or the library. The Fish House was exchanged for a pre-college summer-long workshop at University of Tampa. I took classes in math, language, grammar and composition and then entered St. Petersburg Junior College in the fall of 1968. My pre-med aspirations had given Dad hope; I was his last chance to have another doctor in the family. He paid for everything, although I worked nights during my first semester.

My new night job was great. I worked in a leased department of a large department store. My area specialized in fine jewelry, so I was trained in engraving, small watch repair, and the appraisal and sale of diamonds. My hours accommodated my course schedule, so I worked a fair amount each week.

One evening my father contacted me and told me to get to the hospital; my wife was in labor, two weeks early. It was September twenty-sixth. They told me to stay in the waiting room. For three or four hours I smoked and watched TV. At the time, it was normal for the father and any other visitors to be kept out of the delivery room.

My father, dressed in scrubs, finally appeared with a stuffed white blanket in his arms. For shear shock value, he came close to me and opened the blankets: the baby was still covered in blood and birth fluids. Dad unabashedly spread the legs apart so I could see it was a girl. "You are a father now. Grow up! Start thinking about someone beside yourself," Dad said as he walked off.

Helen and I had agreed to name her Veronica. Veronica Lee Patton, I repeated to myself in disbelief. A few minutes later, a nurse brought her out all cleaned up and modestly wrapped in a pink blanket. She handed my daughter to me with a congratulatory, "Here Dad, she's healthy and beautiful."

This was reality. I fell in love immediately. Little did I know this tiny girl was to influence my life in the most positive and unimaginable ways. Nor could I have envisioned the path my life would take.

Eight – Flee Youthful Lusts

Big results require big ambitions.
Heraclitus

E ven after getting married, I gave in to my buddies occasionally and
went out for a night of drinking and carousing. Obviously, this did
not please Helen.

After Veronica was born, Mom and Dad left for Vinita, Oklahoma
where he was to take a new job as Chief of Medical and Clinical Surgery
at Northeastern State Mental Hospital. The superintendent, B.F. Peterson,
graduated with Dad and knew Mom as well. They were given a comfortable
home on the grounds and a great salary for my father. My little family
remained in the homestead in St. Petersburg, along with my sister, her
husband Bob, and their infant son.

Patty was in touch with our folks concerning my schoolwork and
general behavior. Before I finished my first semester at SPJC, Dad called
and suggested I needed a change of surroundings. With my parents as
residents of the state, I could get lower fees at a college in Oklahoma—and
make new friends.

The day after my last class, my parents arrived in St. Pete to help Helen
and me pack and follow them the one-thousand miles back to Vinita in our
turquoise Volkswagen Bug. We took turns holding Veronica in the back
seat, first in one car and then the other.

We all settled into the warm brick home. Helen learned to play bridge—she always partnered with Mom who was patient and really knew the game. Dad played by the seat of his pants, had little patience, became angry from time to time, and cheated a bit—his only vice I was aware of.

Just after Christmas, I began my first and only semester at Oklahoma A&M. The college was thirty-five miles northeast of Vinita, which required traveling on famous Route 66—a two-lane road with nothing but barb-wired, flat, cow pastures for scenery before reaching U.S. #19 and my destination .

Without the influence of wild friends, drugs and drinking, I apparently matured somewhat and was more motivated than I had been at SPJC. My grades improved from 1.69 the first semester to 2.93 the second. And the courses at A&M were more difficult.

To be eligible for medical school, I had to have a degree from a university so I transferred to Northeastern Oklahoma State University for my remaining undergraduate semesters.

The school was founded in 1851, as the Cherokee National Seminary. In 1906, it became Northeastern State College—the oldest institution of higher learning in Oklahoma as well as one of the oldest located west of the Mississippi River. The main campus of what is now Northeastern Oklahoma State University is located in Tahlequah, the Capitol of the Cherokee Nation in the foothills of the Ozark Mountains. The small classes staffed by a great faculty, and the beautiful campus with large trees and one-hundred-sixty-year-old buildings scattered among the new, fed my ambitions. Our living on campus was another motivating factor.

Previously, I had tiptoed through or audited easy math courses, as math seemed to be my nemesis. When I was faced with mathematics prerequisites for physics, a pre-med requirement, I was delighted to meet a professor who had come up through the ranks as a seasoned high school math teacher. Dr. Stone opened my mind and found the switch. *All* the mathematics I had ever been exposed to was now conceptually at my mental fingertips—everything became clear as crystal. What I later came to know as a hypo-manic episode lasted an entire semester.

After first making my way through four additional math courses, I could do the Physics mid-term exam mostly in my head, using Newton's calculus. I turned in the paper in about five minutes. Professor Galloway glanced at it, "Math major, eh?"

I made an A in the course and any other math courses I took. Organic Chemistry was impossible, however. Dropping Organic wiped out my previous success on the Medical Aptitude Test and the assurance I would be accepted at Dad's alma mater, University of Tennessee Medical School.

The morning I dropped Organic, I had just come from the maternity ward where I saw my baby boy, Sebastian, for the first time. I was proud to have a son. Now being the father of two kids, I reconsidered the many years of education before me. I had to tell Dad I wanted to change my major to mathematics. His response was kind and gentle, "Whatever makes you happy, Bud."

From the very outset of our marriage, out of boredom I'm sure, Helen occupied herself with television soap operas. Living vicariously through these dramas, she began to suspect me unjustly. She was obsessed with order when it came to housekeeping; I was not, making it hard on both of us.

She may have married me because I was an exciting delinquent teenager who offered a way out of her strict home environment. I was a 135 lb. average looking guy—she was downright beautiful. Keeping the house, watching TV, and the burden of the kids—only fourteen months apart and admittedly a bundle to care for—must have been depressing for her. And the pregnancies had scarred her lovely figure.

We did not agree on methods of discipline. If I even hinted I was concerned about her approach, we had a raging argument. To my mind, she was abusing our children. Perhaps it was a way to punish me. I was no angel; indeed, I was selfish and prideful and refused to find something in common with my wife or to search for ways to show my love for her. There were times when I simply left to go to the library to study, or to the river to drink and fish, hoping I might return with a more forgiving or understanding attitude.

Since we spent most weekends at my parents, my mom helped with the kids while Dad took every occasion to admonish Helen as he observed her handling of the children. This made for a horrible time for us all. One weekend Helen simply got up and left to walk the seventy miles back to Tahlequah; she did so—with the help of an occasional ride.

At the beginning of my last semester in the fall of 1971, Helen and I had the worst of our many arguments. This one concerned both my drinking and how she disciplined the children. This time she called her parents in Florida, then turned to me and threatened to take the kids and leave.

Patty and Bob had moved to Tahlequah a year or so before so Bob could complete his BS in Business Administration. At this point, our two apartments faced each other. I went next door to tell my sister what was happening and we agreed we should call Dad. He came immediately, with a stop at the Tahlequah courthouse. When he showed up at Patty's he had a restraining order, a temporary custody judgment in my favor, and two deputies to remove the kids from Helen.

Veronica, Sebastian and I moved in with Patty, Bob, and their two children. All the children were close in age and they kept my sister jumping. Patty exhibited the same personality traits as my mom, offering love and understanding to all four children.

When Helen's parents arrived two days later, my fear of an ensuing court battle heightened and then quickly vanished—they left the next day with only Helen and her belongings.

My family of three stayed with Patty and Bob for the remainder of my final semester. Immediately after graduation I enrolled in the winter semester of graduate school at Oklahoma State University in Stillwater, over one-hundred-fifty miles from my sister's family and my folks.

I had Veronica and Sebastian with me; one in diapers, one in training pants. I had to find a way to care for them and to attend classes at the same time.

I started with only three mathematics courses, so I was not away from my kids more than an hour-and-a-half at a time, when I took them to a student daycare center. I loved my children and hugged and kissed them constantly. I avoided yelling and spanking; I sent them to their room for thirty minutes when I thought discipline was necessary.

Occasionally, a coed from the neighborhood would knock on the door to introduce herself and satisfy her curiosity concerning my family situation. Yes, I was a single dad. I started getting homemade dinners, and then meals cooked at my house, and sometimes even a sleep over or two.

Nine – Get a Real Job

Life grants nothing to us mortals without hard work.
Horace

After eight months, Helen called and asked to come back; I replied with a clear "No way."

The calls continued and we began to tell each other about our lives: she in St. Pete, and I in Stillwater, at OSU. We talked a little longer each time she called. She seemed apologetic and even contrite. This positive side of her had never surfaced before. I asked myself, why does she want to come back? I didn't believe it was for my sake *or* the kids. I remained skeptical: of necessity she was still living with her parents

In spite of my doubts, guilt finally prevailed. After all, I had indulged in multiple affairs since her departure, had been a poor husband and become a professional student supported entirely by my father. I sent a plane ticket to Helen to fly from St. Petersburg to Tulsa, where we stayed the night before the drive to Stillwater. The kids seemed happy to see their mom and I noticed her treatment of the children seemed better.

I left OSU after the one semester; I had to postpone working toward my master's degree and earn some money. My first job was digging postholes and stretching barbed wire fence. The work in the Oklahoma heat was almost unbearable; it was as tough as it had been at the Fish House.

I decided to take the Civil Service Exam, and while waiting on the results, I applied for a teaching position in St. Louis, Missouri. I was interviewed and then hired for the school year to begin in September of '72. We said goodbye to my folks, Patty and Bob and their kids, and moved in a U-Haul truck to Pacific, Missouri, near St. Louis.

While waiting for the school year to begin, I worked as a security guard at Six Flags over Mid America. I became enamored with sixteen-year old Susie, an ice cream girl; I was only twenty-one. She was riding on the back of my motorcycle when we slid off a curve on a downhill road. I was driving too fast and we hit a spot of gravel, throwing us straight into a small rock cliff just off the road. She had only a skinned knee, but I experienced excruciating pain in my lower back. I had fractured three transverse processes in consecutive lumbar vertebrae and crushed two discs. The bike was in good enough shape to get Susie home. I lost the pain; shock I supposed. At least I wasn't charged with statutory rape, but I did spend the next four weeks in bed, racked with pain. Don't tell me God doesn't save and punish his wayward children. I never saw Susie again; my injuries healed just in time to start my teaching job.

The big move was behind us and I was immersed in teaching when in October I finally received my civil service rating: a GS-9 and an offer for a position in a weapons laboratory as a cryptographer. Although very intriguing, moving to Golden, Colorado just didn't fit into my career plans. The salary for the government would have been about $9,000. My teaching job paid $6,800 plus another $1,000 for driving a school bus. We took out a mortgage on a nice, four-year-old, three-bedroom and two-bath house for only $18,000. We had a basement and an enclosed garage and the house sat on an acre of land in the country. (Three years later, my second sailboat cost more than our house.)

One weekend I went on a drinking binge with two friends; I hardly remember going into St. Louis and nightclub hopping. When I returned home with the help of my neighbor's wife, whom I had met somewhere during my travels that weekend, Helen, the kids, the car, and all personal belongs were gone. She was driving to St. Petersburg; I didn't blame her.

It was my turn to call and beg to come home. After multiple promises, I resigned my teaching job at the end of the first semester, put the house up for sale with a realtor, sold my bike for a car, and made for St. Pete.

We stayed with Helen's parents for a few weeks—they said very little to me—until I landed another teaching job at Nathan Gibbs High School. With Dad's blessing, we moved the renters from our family home so we could move in. My second semester mathematics assignment at Gibbs, which had been an all-black school, was an experience. White kids were being bused in from the "Rebel Flag" High School.

At the end of the school year I spent the summer installing chain link fence. I could not handle the problems at Gibbs High so I took another teaching job at Clearwater Central Catholic High School, good Protestant though I was. I taught there for a full year.

Just before completing my master's degree, I was asked to interview for an administrative position with the Manatee County School Board, just north of Sarasota. I was awarded the job with the help of my friend, Joe, who was leaving the position. Joe and I were working together at the University of South Florida in the combined Urban Research Masters/ Doctoral program

In July of 1974, the thirty-three schools in the district had a student population of thirty-two thousand and a budget of $357 million; it is easily double that now. My formal title was Director of Measurement, Research and Instructional Data Processing. This was a fancy title for my job responsibilities: overseeing all testing, program evaluation, research, running and programming a thirty-two terminal computer system as it related to instructional support, budgeting—and later in the early '80s, coordinating the new microcomputer resources. It seemed my ship had come in.

This job became my only security for almost twelve years. I had received tenure after the first three, so in spite of events in my personal life and the eventual lengthy absences for illness, my familiar squeaky desk chair was always there waiting for me. I had a building of my own with a secluded office suite in the back area nestled between a large computer room, the staff area and the lobby. An elevator went down to a warehouse of myriad test instruments.

I was filled with gratitude and a sense of professional achievement; although I didn't feel I deserved it. Working by day and commuting to the University of South Florida nights, I completed my Master's Degree in December of 1975 and continued in the Doctoral Program.

PART TWO – First Onset

1973-1987

Ten – Insanity?

I doubt if a single individual could be found from the whole of mankind free from some form of insanity. The only difference is one of degree.
Desiderius Erasmus

In my early teens, I experienced strange mental phenomena while experimenting with hallucinogens, but I stopped using when I was fifteen. At nineteen, I quit smoking marijuana because it made me paranoid. My only substance abuse for the next ten years involved prescribed amphetamines for weight loss during my college days, and the casual use of alcohol. Could any of this be having an effect on me now that I was an adult? My brain and mind had since functioned effectively: I'd earned two degrees in mathematics.

What happened in late 1973 was not a flashback or anything related to the few times I had used drugs; I was completely sober, and had been for months.

I was driving my car and all seemed normal, when suddenly my mind went blank and I didn't know where I was or where I was going. A few seconds later, my brain began speaking to me too rapidly, randomly, and unintelligibly. I felt as though a tape recorder in my brain was running in fast rewind.

An undergraduate psychology professor had once stated in class, "The primary reason for people 'going insane' was the very *fear* of going insane."

I had never experienced such terror. It seemed to go on forever while I continued to drive subconsciously. The seconds were like hours and the minutes seemed like days. Thoughts of a timeless eternal hell came and went quickly through my mind and a powerful urge compelled me to drive even faster and end my life up against a passing power pole. I came damn close to suicide.

I don't remember getting home, but once there I did have the sense to medicate myself into oblivion with a quart of Jim Beam—the only "psychiatric" medication I had or knew of at the time. I drank until I passed out.

Waking many hours later, I was never so happy to have the familiar mindset of a hangover. Memory of the horror of this attack followed me for months, accompanied by the fear that it could happen again. What method of suicide would I have to prevent next time?

I never sought or received any treatment after this first, but not last, mental aberration of that kind. The Roman Catholics had had an effect on me. When I was teaching mathematics at Clearwater Central Catholic High School, a friendly priest explained to me the legitimate use of exorcism and showed me the rites in his Roman Bible. I'd been exceedingly disturbed by the movie *The Exorcist*, and now, more than ever, I believed in demons. My emotions ruled as I contemplated all that had happened. Within three months, however, my mind once again gained the upper hand.

Although I continued to fear a relapse, I was able to function normally. I experienced the blues from time to time, but in between I was normal or filled with unusual feelings of excitement that allowed me to work wonders with anything I set my mind to. These mood swings just seemed typical; didn't everyone have their ups and downs?

The week prior to Christmas of 1976 my eldest brother, Ralph, came from Milwaukee for a weeklong cruise in my newest sailboat, the LuLu Belle, with me and my six-year-old son. I had just received my Master's Degree in Educational Measurement and Statistics from the University of South Florida. Now I hoped to impress my brother further with my large, sleek new boat, so I stocked it with bottles of premium liquor and food. The three of us left the Yacht Club only an hour before dusk. I was in an increasingly excited mood; I hadn't slept for two days. As the sun set, we approached Egmont Key at the mouth of Tampa Bay. An eerie, dense fog settled in and when we could no longer see the island, I dropped and set the anchor.

The only salient points of conversation I can recall concerned a bottle of Grand Marnier, which I presented as "grand mariner"—thinking it would demonstrate some appropriate class. In a condescending manner, Ralph told me it was pronounced like the French—"Marn-yay"—or something of that sort. Then, when I put Mussorgsky's *Pictures at an Exhibition* in the stereo, I was corrected; the composer's name was not "Moserosky." I felt humbled by my big brother, who had always been more refined.

We ate and drank, then went to our bunks anticipating an offshore sail south to Sarasota after our breakfast coffee. I could not sleep until early morning and then I slept only long enough to have a either a dream or spiritual vision I've never forgotten. I don't think my nocturnal activities bothered Ralph until sometime later in the trip.

We started with a five-to-ten knot breeze, but by midmorning a strong nor'easter began to build. These twenty-to-thirty knot winds were not uncommon during winter months and could continue for days. Since we were headed south, I ran the sails in a broad reach, almost downwind. After a time, the waves joined the wind, cresting to six feet. We were moving at boat speed; this was why I loved sailing. Apparently, my behavior, conversation, and the weather began to concern Ralph more than I perceived.

I decided that Venice was too far to reach before nightfall. The only other navigable inlet before that was Big Sarasota Pass. I knew an anchorage just inside the pass where we could enjoy the lee side of Bird Key.

Adjusting for an easterly course, I warned I had to bring the boat into a beat, which would cause the boat to lean heavily to starboard. The boat was heeling between twenty and thirty degrees. My son was completely at ease enjoying the wet course we were now following; Ralph was not. He voiced his concern, but he hadn't begun yelling at me yet.

I assured him I knew what I was doing; we kept this course for forty-five minutes until we reached the lee side of Lido Key. The wind and surf were now quiet in comparison to only a few minutes before. We tacked up Little Sarasota Bay to the nice quiet anchorage and I think the first thing on Ralph's mind was a stiff drink.

It was some time before I learned my euphoric delusions of grandeur and reckless behavior, among other symptoms, could be frightening to those around me. I just felt more and more exhilarated and had no reason to think I was not making sense. These mere mortals, blathering on, did not deter me.

After another night of my not sleeping, Ralph said, "I've had enough." The plan had been to go offshore again and make the Venice Yacht Club in half a day. Instead, with the northerly wind still strong, we tacked up Sarasota Bay. I ran aground ordering a tack too close to the channel marker. I told Ralph we weren't hard aground. If we were, I would have to swim to the middle of the channel with the anchor on a boat cushion and then use a winch to pull the boat out. Both Sebastian and Ralph would have had to climb out to the tip of the boom so the boat would incline and draw less. He was happy when I solved the problem using the wind, the sail, our inboard and the tiller. We were again on our way.

When we approached the Ringling Causeway on a hard starboard tack, I passed the point of no return and the bridge had just started to go up. Ralph seemed amazed when my mast passed through a four-foot wide gap with at least ten feet of mast towering above the span. I was showing off but I could have wrecked my boat.

We continued up the open water of the large Sarasota Bay until the tossing, turning, loosing and winching sail took its toll on my crew. Reluctantly I started the inboard and headed for a crab restaurant on Longboat Key, where I knew we could get Ralph's feet on solid ground.

Ralph and Sebastian never got back aboard. After rescuing my boat from my haphazard docking—which had caused the boat to drift several hundred yards from the dock—we caught a ride home. I returned the next day with a friend to help me sail back to the Club.

I had not had but a few hours' sleep in five days. Ralph stayed at my house for a couple of days until I could drive him fifteen miles north to his in-laws, where his family joined him for the holiday. Ralph seemed very upset with me. He stopped short of yelling at me at the top of his lungs, but he hassled me endlessly for what seemed no good reason at the time. His reaction was not enough to get me hospitalized. It was my in-laws and my wife who convinced me, after I had gone seven days without sleep, to let them take me to St. Anthony's Hospital.

Eleven – The Psych Ward

The fires of a supreme zest for living and the most gnawing desire for death alternate in my heart, sometimes in the course of a single hour.
Gustav Mahler

So the Romans had me again in December 1976. The Catholic hospital, a seven-story building, boasted a huge neon cross on the top, which was visible from the courtyard of the psychiatric ward.

The diagnosis: Schizophrenia, and the prognosis was not good. Dr. H divined a drug cocktail that left me hallucinating all night long, even though I had not slept for over a week. When he interviewed me, I told him of my recent experiences. With the Physician's Desk Reference in hand, he flipped pages until he came up with a different concoction of pharmaceuticals. I finally slept that night and when I awoke, there was a noticeable decrease in the excited state that had been building in me for over a week.

I began to drool, my neck stiffened and my scalp crawled. Dr. H. said that was normal, but added still another drug. He said, "This will correct the problem." It didn't. Each day of my three-week stay, I became less and less excited, eventually leaving me with two goals: to sleep for hours on end and to skip meals. I had no interest in the other patients, even those I had become friends with and had enjoying talking to—especially one young pretty girl with deep scars on her wrists. She was a strange gothic-type individual who talked incessantly. When I was finally released to Helen, these new, dark, depressive symptoms continued for weeks.

I returned home the day before my mom and dad left the ship where he now served as ship's physician for Norwegian Caribbean Lines. He had completed one of his three-month tours. My life had caused my mom great emotional stress—she was the epitome of "mothers go where angels fear to tread." Ever since she first learned I was in a mental ward, Mom had pleaded with Dad to take off time so she could see me, but he waited until his tour was up.

I had a small two-bedroom apartment available for them to use as home base while they traveled some during their month-long leaves from the ship. When they arrived this time, we had a wonderful reunion. They hugged and spoiled their grandchildren, Sebastian now six years old and Veronica, seven.

We played a little bridge until I became groggy from my meds. Our duplex apartment was adjacent to theirs, so I returned to our side, lay on the couch, and listened to the sound of Mom's organ coming through the wall. She was playing Bach's *Toccata* and *Fugue in D-minor.* I fell asleep, waking just long enough to feel her give me a kiss goodnight.

Around six a.m., I heard Dad beating on the front door. "Something's the matter with your mother!" he yelled, as he turned to run back next door. I followed close behind. There was Mom lying face up on the bed. I hurried to attempt CPR as Dad cried hysterically, "Do something Roddy—do something!"

She was obviously already gone. I searched for the Bible I'd left for them in their apartment, but I couldn't find it, so I just sank to my knees and repeated what I'd so often heard from my Grandmother: "The Lord is my shepherd…."

It provided no comfort. I cursed God. Dad was in a heap on the floor. "You're the doctor—*you* do something!" I screamed. When the EMS people arrived, both Dad and I yelled at them, faulting them for taking so long.

I don't recall anything about the rest of the day. But for weeks, months, and years afterward, I had a new emotion to deal with—grief so overwhelming that it seemed like a hole in my chest. On top of the grief, I had to cope with the guilt, not from my illness, but from the conviction that I had driven my mom to an early death: she was only sixty-two. My depression became worse and Dad seemed utterly destroyed.

Three weeks later I decided to quit taking all drugs except the Valium and Phenobarbital, two drugs I was familiar with. I was then able to return to the office and attempt working once again.

Anxiety was my constant companion, but the Valium helped. My father, in an effort to save me some money, had purchased pharmacy bottles of five-hundred tablets of 10mg Valium, a thousand of 100mg Phenobarbital, large bottles of Haldol—which I hated—and something called Cogentin. I tolerated Valium easily and had to take ten tablets to get the buzz I needed to keep working. My self-medicating, or in this case selective drug abuse, included alcohol.

"Oh I get by with a little help from my friends, Mmm, I get high with a little help from my friends, Mmm, I'm gonna try with a little help from my friends." Song by Joe Cocker, 1969. Six months went by and the familiar excited mood returned.

One Saturday in August of '77, Helen and I and some bridge-playing friends left the Club for a weekend sail to Bahia Beach Resort. It was a seven-hour sail—under the Skyway Bridge and east to the southern shore of Tampa Bay. We had a great sail, arrived late afternoon, tied up for the night, and went to dinner at a seafood restaurant near the docks. After dinner, we returned to the boat for more drinks and several rubbers of bridge.

By eleven, we retired to our separate cozy bunks. I lay awake for most of the night listening to the contented sounds of sleep from the others, the calls of Whippoorwills, and the gentle lapping of water against the hull.

At daybreak Helen woke and began fixing the coffee and a light breakfast before we got under way. While at full sail, we enjoyed a few Bloody Marys and toasted each other, saying, "I wonder what the poor folks are doing."

As we approached our homeport, I began to experience that familiar high and excited mood. I secured the boat, and we all hugged goodbye. I watched our friends leave the Club in their car. I told Helen I had to clean up the boat, so she left in her car, leaving me there with my bike—my new toy—a 1976 Kawasaki KZ900 road bike. It was my habit to push it as fast as it could go, but safety was always on my mind.

However, after I left the Club, I was in the mood for speed and I felt invincible. I crossed the two-lane bridge from Palmetto to Bradenton at well over a hundred miles and hour, riding the yellow line with traffic on either side Then I did the same going east on Manatee Avenue, the main street of the city, quickly approaching the bike's top speed and paying no attention to red lights. I sped from 9th Street to 51st, at least forty-two blocks.

I turned left on 51st Street, a more lightly traveled road, and let go with complete abandon. When I realized I should have been on 59th Street, I turned off onto a vacant lot filled with sand and small shrubs to span the eight blocks.

Until my early twenties I had raced motocross, but now I was not on a dirt bike. Despite the sliding, jumping, and swerving to avoid the bushes I still held my speed—70mph at least. Then as if God Himself was yelling over the roar of the engine, I heard a clear shout, "STOP!"

I laid the bike down and slid about ten feet. When I stood up I was awestruck to see a twenty-foot-deep chasm—over fifty-feet across—with scores of iron rebar embedded in the concrete sticking up five feet and aimed directly at me.

Given the speed and curve of the arc I would have made had I not stopped, four or five of the lethal spears would have impaled me like a phalanx of attacking Spartans. No doubt whatsoever: I would have been killed instantly.

I was looking at a large storm drain under construction for a planned gated subdivision. I had raced over ten miles in less than seven minutes. Stunned, I left the bike there as it began to rain, clambered down the abyss of my would-be death, emerged up on the other side, and walked the few blocks home.

When I arrived I told Helen, without hesitation, to take me back to the hospital.

Twelve – Emotional Reasoning

I do not feel obliged to believe that the same God who has endowed us with sense, reason, and intellect has intended us to forgo their use.
Galileo Galilei

The neon cross seemed a comfort as I entered the familiar ward. The only change in six months was a completely new set of patients. My doctor was still there. He remained of the opinion I was schizophrenic. I find it difficult to articulate my feelings to psychiatrists. First, the questions asked don't lend themselves to cognitive answers. Secondly, I don't think they really listen: It's all guesswork, trial and error.

I had concluded taking Haldol was a problem for me. I told him of my symptoms and admitted I stopped taking the prescribed medications immediately after my last discharge. I also related my experiences that lead to both this and my first admittance. He started me on another brew of drugs. I recognized only the Phenobarbital and Valium among all the other meds I took from the paper cup three times a day.

Although I was somewhat anxious and paranoid, I enjoyed the food and sleep. I have no memory of what precipitated the event, but I suddenly found myself locked in a small room with thick leather straps and cuffs holding my hands and feet almost immovable.

A nurse came in only to administer meds and to bring me food. I could barely touch my fingers together so I could eat. I lost track of the days; each one seemed to pass by so slowly because I was losing by ability to sleep.

What took place next, I remember as though it happened yesterday. As unbelievable as it seemed, I was filled with strength and consumed with anger. I tried to remove my wedding band. When Helen first placed it on my finger, I weighed 135 pounds; I was now two-twenty. I became obsessed with the task and refused to give up. Use of my fingers was severely limited, so I finally removed the ring with my teeth. As soon as I spit the ring to the far corner of the room, the anger left and the adrenaline-rush ceased.

I struggled to pull my hands out of the cuffs. Within minutes, I succeeded. With the strength of my now-free hands, I was able to remove the foot cuffs as well. I retrieved the ring, forced it back on my finger, and then walked to the door to look out. To my surprise, I could open it. Had the door been locked? Probably not.

I walked through the door and to the right, away from the main ward where people were milling around. I came to another door at the end of the hall, opened it and walked through it as well, into a room filled with medical supplies. I noticed shelves holding everything from syringes to medication. Surely, this door would have been kept locked. How did I get through? I approached another door; again I walked through. This larger room contained medical equipment such as X-Ray and EKG machines. Wouldn't this door have been locked?

As I moved I was filled with over-whelming emotions and a delusion of grandeur, feeling first emboldened and then invincible. I was convinced I had walked through three locked doors. When I reached what proved to be last next door, as I expected, I was able to open it and pass through. When I did, I found myself outside of the psych ward and inside the main part of the hospital.

Recalling the strange phenomenon associated with my drug experiences as a teenager, I knew I had witnessed stranger happenings, and so I had no fear. Obsessed with my power and filled with an alien glee, I was propelled to the only entrance to the psych ward. I pressed the entrance button; in a few seconds a nurse came to the door. The procedure was for her to signal to the glass-enclosed nurses' station if she approved the caller; they would then open the door.

When the nurse saw me through the window, I could see the look of terror on her face before she turned to run back to the nurses' station. I wasn't sure what she thought she saw, but, wickedly, I enjoyed her reaction.

In a few minutes, *all* the nurses came to see for themselves just what was taking place. They appeared as upset as the first nurse and refused to let me in. There were no men on the ward. The nurses talked among themselves, but I couldn't hear what was being said. About ten minutes later, the door was opened and I entered. Like the Red Sea, they parted to allow me through. As I approached the nurses' station, a gruff old nurse whom I called Cleo, spoke up with a trembling voice and asked, "Richard, will you go back to your room?"

"Yes. If you won't strap me to the bed and you won't lock the door."

She agreed. Still walking with Cleo and the other nurses, I returned to the room. As I entered, I heard the door close behind me and the distinct click of a lock. Still I pushed the door open with no effort. Some voice deep inside me angrily roared, "I said NOT to lock the door!"

The gathering scattered and left me standing alone in the doorway. I shut the door and moved to the center of the room. Suddenly an involuntary spasm gripped my body. Every muscle moved as though performing an isometric exercise and I had no power to stop. My body was no longer my own. My brain ran non-stop and offered nothing intelligible for my mind to focus on.

Time stopped for me, but at some point the doctor, two male aids, and Helen came into the room. They laid my stiff body on the bed and gave me a shot.

Several days later, I awoke feeling quite normal and refreshed, but the memory of that terrifying experience still lingered in my mind. Dr. H. called me to his office and explained that I had slipped into a catatonic state. It had been an hour-and-a-half before he could reach Helen to come in and give permission for him to perform Electro Convulsive Therapy. The chart indicated I had lost almost ten pounds of fluid in the meantime.

After two more weeks of taking only Valium and Phenobarbital, I was allowed to leave.

I believe "emotional reasoning" is really an oxymoron, but the rational component of my mind added little to my understanding of events around me.

Thirteen – Ancient Rites

My religion consists of a humble admiration of the illimitable
superior spirit who reveals himself in the slight details we
are able to perceive with our frail and feeble mind.
Albert Einstein

Three days after I returned home, Don and Barbara came by to talk with me. They were friends, but also Bible thumpers. Emotions were still over-ruling my mind, in spite of—or perhaps as a result of—the drugs and alcohol. Helen told my visitors I was in the back yard and that I was drinking.

They came and stood as I sat leaning against the house defiant and somewhat inebriated. I could have done without this at that moment. However, all they said was, "We know someone who may be able to help you. May we pick you up at five tomorrow afternoon? We just want you to meet him."

It couldn't hurt so I responded impolitely, "Sure, I'll go."

Helen, Don and Barbara, and I drove to the countryside east of Bradenton. A strong dose of Valium had calmed me and my mind seemed vacant. I didn't say a word.

We pulled into a large compound surrounding an immense cathedral. After we entered the tabernacle, we quickly turned into a small, furnished side room. A middle-aged man introduced himself to Helen, acknowledged our friends with a cheerful greeting of familiarity. They spoke among themselves for a moment, beyond my hearing. The man asked me to get comfortable on the couch, without mentioning my name.

Then to my astonishment he held a cross too close to my face and after saying, "In the name of Jesus, identify yourself," he began a diatribe against me

I was instantly transported into a catatonic state similar to the one I had in the hospital only weeks before. I couldn't move: I couldn't speak. I could only assimilate a diminutive amount of what was said as he attacked me verbally; it seemed to go on forever. Helen told me later she thought it had been about forty-five minutes.

Suddenly, in a very meek voice he addressed me by name and asked if I was all right. I felt as I had in the hospital when I awakened after the ECT, but I was still trembling. I answered his question with "Yes," then immediately asked if I could go outside for a cigarette.

We drove home silently as I wrestled emotionally with what had just taken place. Had this been an intense psychological phenomenon, or a medieval religious spoof perpetrated on a quite unwilling subject? Multiple drinks and even more doses of drugs followed this event.

A few days later I started out on my bike, headed for the Yacht Club to have a few drinks and fellowship with those of my sailing friends who were of the same mind at the same time. Instead, when I reached Palmetto, I decided to provoke the pastor of the First Baptist Church with some in-depth, emotional reasoning in a discussion about religion.

Sally, the Church Secretary, was the wife of Vernon, my closest coworker at the School Board. This was their church, so when I asked Sally if I could see the pastor, she went to get him immediately. A large muscular man came from his study into the lobby and introduced himself. My impression, in spite of my ever-present confusion, was that he exhibited the same character and personality as my friend, Vernon.

First let me tell you about Vernon. He was all action, no words—a true disciple, and testament of a good man in all respects.

On one occasion in Tallahassee, he and I were enjoying a meal at the Hilton a few blocks from the Capitol House where we were working. I got drunk and tried to make a date with a waitress. She probably bragged to her boyfriend at the bar, saying something like, "See, there are other guys interested in me."

He was drunk, too; we fought each other and tore the place apart. Vernon went to the manager and asked him not to call the police. In addition, he said he was my attorney and assured him that reparation would be made. Amazingly Vernon never mentioned the incident back at the office. He was becoming a big brother, but never once rebuked me for my actions.

And now I was attacking his pastor. The big man patiently answered all the questions I put forth—no matter how aggressive I became. In the end, he had my promise to attend church that Sunday.

Fourteen – Religion or Emotion?

*If you board the wrong train, it is no use running along
the corridor in the other direction.*
Dietrich Bonhoeffer

I have learned the first step of a *12-Step Program* requires me to admit I am powerless and my life has become unmanageable—and the second is to *believe* that a Power greater than myself can restore me to sanity. Believing was always the hard part for me. I was unaware at the time, however, that the mind needs to understand it as *reason* in the metaphysical intelligence, rather than as an *emotional* reaction.

On Sunday, August 28, 1977, I sat with Helen in the balcony of the First Baptist Church. I had attended many churches, hundreds of times. How would this be different?

I listened to the sermon in my highly emotional state and learned that to repent meant to turn around and go in the opposite direction—and believe that Christ is my higher power. I always thought to repent meant to stop doing bad things. Here was step two again; too much believing for me. Then they began to sing the invitational hymn for those who would come forward to accept Christ.

The music was beautiful, but the words were haunting. There were only two strains to the melody and it seemed to go on and on. I caved in and responded. The experience was cathartic, requiring no thought at all.

Walking down to the altar was the most humiliating experience I've ever had. Many of those present worked for the school board and I was sure they knew of my shameful, promiscuous reputation and notoriety for being a supercilious, foolish drunk.

When the pastor took my hand, I wept and no words would come. The incessant hymn stopped and he presented me to the congregation as a new believer, who would be baptized at the evening service.

A never-ending line of members formed and praised God because of my *decision*. Even though I recognized most of the people from various work relationships, I didn't sense any condemnation. Instead, they emitted an aura akin to that of my friend, Vernon.

After church Helen prepared a lamb roast—of all things—for dinner. My emotions reeled, but in a good way. My mind was still in the ozone.

I became increasingly agitated, but still had a positive outlook. When it came time for the evening service, delusions set in and I anticipated a grand happening. I had not slept at all since the visit to the pastor's office the Wednesday before.

The large, old church was as packed with congregants as it had been that morning. Did they all return to see if I would go through with it?

Helen brought along some shorts and a tee shirt for me to change into before the baptism. As this was a Baptist church, I was to be completely immersed. After changing in the back of the church, I donned a white robe. I was told I had only to cross my arms and hold my nose: the pastor would do the rest.

Others were to undergo the Sacrament: I was third in line and could observe the process. Then it was my turn. The pastor spoke loudly to me so the congregation could hear as well. From what I remember, he asked several questions, to which I answered in the affirmative. He then said, "I baptize you Richard in the Name of the Father, the Son and the Holy Spirit. Enter into Christ's death."

I plunged backward into the cold water and when he pulled me back up he said, "You have passed from death and risen to a new life." I dried off, changed, but did not return to Helen and the kids who were seated in the sanctuary.

I walked outside and wandered around the church before noticing a dark and foreboding funeral parlor across the street. I decided to brazenly knock on the door and persisted until an angry-looking gentleman came out to see who required his services at 8:30 in the evening. I told him I had just died and was in need of a coffin. He stormed back inside, mumbling something about the police.

The Palmetto police arrived just as the church service was over and people were filing out. Vernon was among them, and when he saw the police he immediately thought of me. He spoke to the officers and they left. Vernon was well known and trusted in Palmetto. This was the second time he kept me out of jail.

When we arrived home, I was euphorically psychotic. Despite doses of Valium and Phenobarbital, I couldn't sleep and kept Helen awake, too. Early the next morning Vernon came to the house and asked, "Are you ready to go?"

I now considered him a trusted brother; his silence concerning my behavior had earned my obedience. I didn't ask where we were going, but quickly agreed in hopes of another adventure.

While we drove, he told me the superintendent wanted to keep me in my position regardless of my illness. The official story had been that I had blood pressure problems, and the story would remain the same. Vernon confirmed my growing fear. "You have to get well. I'm taking you to get help."

Once inside the hospital they offered me a wheelchair. Vernon nodded to me that I should take it. Then they bound me with the familiar constraints for my hands and feet. I looked to Vernon as butterflies became bats in my stomach. He placed a small Bible in my lap and said, "Here's your light saber, Luke." He left assuring me he would look in on me frequently.

I was wheeled in to a psychotherapy session just starting, and placed into the perimeter of the circle. A psychiatrist was leading the group. In a certain mood, I am very talkative and show no regard for the feelings of others. I'm also very quick-witted; everything has a funny side intending to embarrass those in authority.

Apparently I won the battle with my insolence and succeeded in making the doctor look like an idiot. But I lost the war. He had me removed from the group, placed in a small windowless room, and strapped to a bed. This was too familiar; it was punitive and had no therapeutic purpose. He left me there for more than a week, with no medicine and no visitors allowed.

The panic attacks kept coming and going; I couldn't sleep. A person in a room on the other side of the wall constantly made noises, sometimes growling and often screaming. I imagined a demon in that room and at the top of my voice began singing all the religious songs I knew. When I asked the aide to bring me my Bible and cross, he came back with a stack of National Geographic magazines and a message from the doctor. "He said you don't need that crap." At least I got an extra smoke from the aide.

Loneliness was my only companion, so whenever I heard the aide selecting a key from his chain, I hoped he was coming to my door. When he entered, he sat on the bed while I smoked and talked. I had no concept of time, day, night, or what meal I was eating. They say that every time his master leaves him, a dog thinks it will be forever. I think that's right.

It must have been the eighth or ninth day when the door opened and in walked the aide, two psychiatrists, a nurse, and two deputy sheriffs. They circled my bed, filling the small room.

The psychiatrist, looking like a king ready to read a declaration to a condemned man, read from what looked like a sheet of legal or charting paper. I could hear the sarcasm in his voice. He said, "We can do nothing for you here. You're diagnosed as a schizophrenic and hyper-religious. You are hereby remanded to the State Mental Hospital. Do you understand? Have any questions?"

The deputies were to be my escort. Anything's better than here, I thought. I have yet to find "hyper-religious" in the *Diagnostic and Statistical Manual of Mental Disorders*.

Fifteen – Across the River Styx

All hope abandon, ye who enter here!
Dante Alighieri

When I entered the ward, the wall was the first thing to get my attention; it was smeared with filthy spots of what appeared to be various body fluids. This hideous canvas was covered with hand-scratched signs—varying from a cross to a pentagram, familiar vulgarities, and individual words such as Jesus, die, help.

I began to examine the wall in more detail, but was overcome as people pushed into me, eager to see the newcomer. Among the crowd was a large, dumb-looking man with a long, sutured scar from the top of his nose up into his scalp. Do they still do prefrontal lobotomies on people, I wondered? Shock therapy, or ECT was something done in the past, I thought. I had already been exorcised. Were they now going to bleed me, cover me with leeches, or burn me at the stake?

A young teenager stood in the milieu. His head appeared twice as large as normal for a person of his size. He made gestures as he spoke—one minute in a normal tone and the next in a deep guttural voice—seeming to answer the question he had just posed.

Suddenly a young man with bright blue, lucid eyes—unlike the dull, vacant look of the others—held out his hand as if he wanted shake mine.

As I took his hand, he gazed into my eyes as if he were looking into my very soul. "Are you Jesus Christ?" he asked.

I immediately let go of his hand and almost screamed, "No! Get away from me!" How long would I be here before I, too became a lunatic? Was this Hell?

The blue-eyed man took off running the seventy-five yards from one end of the ward to the other, ramming his body into the brick wall at the end of each run. He continued for almost twenty minutes before an aide interrupted his television viewing to grab the young man, throw him onto a bedspring with no mattress, and strap him down.

I watched the helpless man writhe and wrestle with the straps, the strength of his effort moving the bedsprings across the floor. He began foaming at the mouth; loud and unusual noises emanated from his throat, adding to the cacophony of the scene.

It all came to a halt when a 280-pound aide in cowboy boots and hat sprang up from his chair, straddled the patient, and strangled him until he passed out. The furious aide got off the bed and addressed all of us who were watching. "The kid will be all right."

During this melee, I heard my name called out. Someone directed me to the phone. My sister Patty was on the line. I cannot recall any of the conversation; I was panic stricken by that point. But the entire episode led to a thought: Maybe I was just in purgatory and my loved ones were out there giving money to the Pope to lessen my time here. Maybe heaven was still a possibility

As the weeks went by, I could detect the medication was adding to my flight of ideas, delusions, and contributing to a deepening depression. We stood in line to receive our pills in a small paper cup along with a larger cup of water to wash it down—all under the watchful eye of a male nurse. Despite his diligence, I was able to make a show of taking the pills, but then spit them in my hand when I was at my bunk and out of his sight. Even though they were a bit soggy, I hid them in a shoe in my locker. I believed many people became lost in a state-run hospital, spending years there with no chance for release. My stash of meds was my insurance, giving me hope for an early discharge.

The facility was huge; at mess time, three-to-five-hundred patients gathered from several of the many wards. The overworked psychiatrist came to our ward about once a week. Two dozen or more of us sat in a circle and waited for our chance to interact with the doctor, anywhere from twenty seconds to two minutes each time. The doctor was less than helpful; it seemed a useless, perfunctory process.

About two weeks into my stay, an aide came across my stash of pills when he was searching through our lockers. My hopes for an early release were dashed. From then on, the aides searched my mouth with a tongue depressor to be certain I'd washed down the meds with the water.

Minutes slowly turned into hours and hours into nights, which were passed in a fitful sleep that lasted as long as the days. One afternoon, I was sitting on my bed, passing time observing my fellow inmates. I saw a hand on the opaque glass door that lead out from the ward and felt an adrenalin rush, but didn't know why. I walked to the door and placed my own hand on the shadow on the other side of the glass. Instantly, I knew it was my father's hand. When the aide opened the door, I could see Dad's tear-stained face through the bars that separated us.

For the first time in weeks, I had hope. *Dad will get me out of here. He has always pulled me out of trouble before; he will do it again.*

As we spoke together, tears streamed from his eyes—at times, he openly wept. I was numb with guilt as I saw Dad's emotion. "There's nothing I can do, son. You've been committed for the long haul."

"How long do I have to stay here," I asked, gripping his hand.

"I don't know. They won't tell me anything—just that you have to be here."

There seemed no way out; he was here so I hugged him for perhaps the last time, still hoping he would change his mind and find a way to get me out.

Dad left. I sat with the carton of cigarettes he'd brought me, gripped with anxiety. I thought of the bumper sticker I'd once read: "I Feel Much Better, Now That I've Given Up All Hope."

I never said much during the weekly sessions when we were all made to sit in the circle with the doctor. He never asked me a direct question, just the same "How do you feel?" he posed to others. I never answered—there seemed no point in it.

Around the seventh week, when it was my turn in the group, he asked, "You ready to go home, Patton?" I thought it a cruel joke until he repeated the question.

"Yes," I replied guardedly.

"Go call someone to come pick you up and then get your stuff together."

I could hardly believe what I was hearing. With permission to leave, I went to the payphone outside the ward and called Helen collect. She seemed hesitant to take my call. I told her they had released me. She said she'd call the doctor to verify my claim and that I should wait at the payphone to hear back from her.

She brought a girlfriend with her and made the sixty-mile drive to the hospital. As I sat there waiting, I felt like I was the last man to be rescued from shark-infested waters.

Sixteen – Darkness

I felt myself in a solitude so frightful that I contemplated suicide.
Jean-Paul Sartre

The seven-week hospital regimen of various tranquilizers removed any vestige of the short, periodic highs I experienced over the previous two years. In the evenings Helen and the children were home with me. During the weekdays, I was alone. The idea of suicide grew stronger and stronger as the weeks went by.

However, my religious beliefs could be defined; I figured I had a fifty-fifty chance of finding a better place beyond. I kept my eyes fixed on a copper-framed pewter relief of the Last Supper as I gradually convinced myself the Deity would understand.

My job awaited me, I loved my children, I was a member of the Yacht Club, and owned a great sailboat. I had everything I could want. If a genie appeared offering three wishes, I would have said there was nothing I desired, because in my current state the depression made things meaningless.

Now the loneliness was so intense and the intermittent panic so great, nothing could dissuade me from my goal. I was sure there would be no end to this terrifying condition—this was the worst yet.

At the time, I didn't have a firearm. After only four days into my first week back home, I took what remained in the large, half-full bottles of

Valium and Phenobarbital and poured them into a blender. I added a cup or so of vodka to cover the probably four hundred pills and capsules. First, I dulled my senses by guzzling vodka, then set out a chaser of water, and turned on the blender.

Helen was due home shortly, so I gulped down the blue potion, chased it with another shot of Vodka, and then followed it with water. I hurried to get most of it down so I could rinse the blender to keep Helen from suspecting anything. Then I called my friend, Jack, an elementary school principal, and asked if I could come over for a drink. I did not want my kids to see me die.

Helen arrived with Veronica and Sebastian just seconds after I got off the phone with Jack. She could see I had been drinking so she refused to give me the keys to a car. I tried to start my bike, but had no luck, so I grabbed my Dad's keys. He had left his car when he flew to Texas with his new bride, whom he had met on the cruise ship.

The car started, but I was quickly losing my motor coordination; a block away, I ran into a ditch. I burned the rear wheels off the car, but could not get free. With the little of my remaining mind, I reasoned I should get back to the house and get in bed. Helen would be able to tell the kids I died in my sleep.

I learned later what took place after I hit the bed and lost consciousness. Shortly afterwards, Jack's wife, Betty, called and said, "Rich told us he was coming over, but he hasn't arrived." Helen told her I was drunk and in bed. Five minutes later Betty called again, said she had a bad feeling and asked if Helen would check my meds.

I had placed the empty bottles back among the other drugs so they would be out of sight. When Helen found them, she estimated how much I had taken and called two neighbors to come help her. The two guys carried me to the back seat of Helen's car and they drove me to the hospital.

My new psychiatrist, who practiced at the hospital, told me later that my attempt had been successful—I was DOA. They revived me with atropine, an adrenaline shot to the heart and cardiac shock. They had some concern about lack of oxygen to my brain; unfortunately, it had no effect on my mental condition.

Three days later, I awoke in a bright, white room with white curtains on one wall. Everything seemed white. Hell wouldn't be white, would it? I noticed I wasn't strapped in, so I removed the tube in my arm, got up, walked over to the window and tentatively peeked through the curtains. Fifty-Ninth Street. I had accomplished nothing.

I was *not* in the afterlife. More than likely I would be returned to the State Hospital. I moved to the door on the other side of the room. Surely, it would be locked; instead, it opened into a room full of activity, a large nurses' station.

A nurse took me by the arm, led me back to my bed and reattached my intravenous bag. She assured me my doctor would be by shortly. Dr. M, a tall, elderly and kind-looking man entered within the hour. When I asked, he replied, "Yes, I am a psychiatrist."

"Are you religious?" I asked.

"I'm Episcopal," he replied simply.

I didn't know for certain what that meant, but it seemed to make things more hopeful. I had recently learned that my psychiatrist from the Catholic hospital, committed suicide. He tied an anchor to his feet and jumped off his sailing sloop named *Libido*." Can a hopeless person help another hopeless person, *or will they both fall into a ditch?*

Nonetheless, there seemed some comfort in this man: after I described my suicide attempt and reviewed my history, he gave a new diagnosis—manic-depressive. In plain words, he told me this illness had been successfully treated for many years, unlike schizophrenia.

He continued, "Your extreme high moods sometimes accompanied by psychosis, are often mistaken as schizophrenia. The corresponding depression is normal for the disease. I've conferred with your superintendent and his assistant and assured them you will be doing all right in several weeks. We discussed the error in diagnosis and the promise for recovery."

Dr. M explained he would treat me on a regular basis as an outpatient. With this kind of confidence, how could I go wrong?

Lithium Carbonate was my new primary drug. My old friend Valium was also prescribed to get me through any anxiety or panic attacks. Later, because my depression lingered longer than expected, a selective serotonin reuptake inhibitor was added.

When I was discharged my sister, Patty, invited me to fly to Pensacola to visit her, Bob and the kids; God bless her. A week in a different environment helped me become acclimated to some very subtle changes in my mood. I had an emotional illness. I was not out of my mind – at least not all the time.

Seventeen – Back to Work

Most men lead lives of quiet desperation and
go to the grave with the song still in them.
Henry David Thoreau

When I settled back in my squeaky desk chair in early 1978, after a sixteen-week stretch in three different hospitals and in an intensive care unit, I realized I had lost all confidence in myself. Fortunately I had a great staff and the school board had access to a temporary consultant while I was away.

Vernon stopped by daily to see how things were going for me. I didn't try to hide the fact I was spending most of the day reading extraneous subject matter. About the third week after my return, he came to tell me the superintendent wanted me to review the results of a countywide State Student Assessment Test (SSAT) and then write a press release.

Analyzing the data and writing the release was the easy part. I was also asked to present my analysis to the instructional staff: all principals, assistants, and district-level personnel—a crowd of over seventy-five. I never had any trouble addressing a group before. But now?

The superintendent called the day before the meeting and told me no one but Vernon, the assistant superintendent, and he knew about my illness. Then he added, "Please discuss your plans for next fall with the O.R.B.I.T project while you're there."

This additional topic made my speech longer, but it also gave me an opportunity to baffle them with BS should the need arise. My undergraduate speech teacher taught me to have confidence in myself because I was the one in control—and the only one who knew precisely what I was speaking about.

I took a handful of Valium forty-five minutes before the zero hour and puked twice outside the boardroom. Still, Vernon wouldn't let me out of giving my presentation.

I chose to address the O.R.B.I.T—Objective Referenced Bank of Items Tests—topic first. I knew I'd find my footing discussing what we could do to increase our statewide ranking, and how to get it accomplished.

In forty minutes, I finished. I felt like a new man, or rather, like the old one.

I continued to make progress and became more aware of my chemically balanced emotions. I took Lithium religiously and had periodic blood-level tests (SSRI) as well. Valium, however, remained my ace in the hole. I skipped doses to increase my supply, a typical addictive personality behavior. Fear of anxiety and panic attacks remained.

Now that I understood my tendency for a continuum from clinical depression and extreme anxiety to hypo-manic, manic, and psychotic behaviors, I *believed* this was what I had been experiencing all along.

After two years of tolerable behavior—within the confines of common blues and above average high energy, but still always rational—I was almost convinced I was well. I attended church regularly and participated in a weekly Bible study group Vernon started in his home, at my request. My sister, Patty, and her husband attended as well. Their family moved to Bradenton in mid-1978 when Bob had to leave a promising Navy career because of the reduction in military forces during the Carter Administration.

I looked forward to the Bible study and could be counted on to ask many critical questions. I was really a skeptic, and had been since my youth. This lead to passionate discussions, but the other members gently avoided my ill-advised desire for polemic debate. I approached questions in a rational manner; my emotional experience of conversion and baptism no longer held sway for me. Emotion vs. faith—they seemed the same to me. I required something more intellectual, more based on reason. Emotion was my enemy; it was not to be trusted.

As time passed, I realized I wasn't as well as I had thought. My lithium therapy was designed to lessen the extent of the swings from suicidal depression to manic psychosis, but I experienced a range of moods. Occasionally I had the blues, like normal people. I didn't really irritate anyone; I just didn't have any energy. Taking the garbage out was a major effort. Getting out of bed in the morning to face the day was almost impossible.

Other times I became hypomanic for weeks. When I managed to stay at this level, everything was great, but I could slip into full mania at any time. I couldn't distinguish my mood change; I just felt better and more alive. I seemed normal, remained courteous, but had an excess of energy with my thoughts running at a safe but top speed. This was enough to drive to distraction those who were close to me.

When I slipped into the manic phase, people were frightened. I could be euphoric, irritable, wrapped in inflated self-esteem or grandiosity. My need for sleep decreased and I talked excessively. My thoughts raced and I was easily distracted, although intent on some goal-driven effort. I could be sexually inappropriate and often became involved in activities that lead to negative consequences such as embarrassing comments or propositions.

At times I lost contact with reality and had a complete psychotic break—usually after many days without sleep. Afterward I remembered very little, but was told I had hallucinations, was delusional, and exhibited a personality change. In the most severe episodes, my behavior became unusual and often bizarre. Social interaction and even daily life activities were difficult for me.

After Dad died late in January 1979, just two days shy of the anniversary of Mom's death, Patty became my confidant and caretaker when the need arose. Only recently did I learn Mom had asked her to look out for me.

It was hardly a surprise when Helen reached a point where she could not go on. I couldn't blame her.

Eighteen – Divorce

Divorce is probably of nearly the same date as marriage.
I believe, however, that marriage is some weeks the more ancient
Voltaire

We were having dinner at the club on March 21, 1979, our eleventh wedding anniversary, when Helen stated she was not happy.

I had made the mistake of "coming clean" about all my indiscretions up until the time of my baptism two years prior. At the time, I was in the Twelve-step Program and learned to list all those I had harmed and make amends to them all. Since then I had lived decently and had not been out of line. She was still not happy, which provoked my pride. I moved out the next day; I'd been feigning happiness myself.

For the sake of the kids, I hoped being apart would give us both time to reassess our marriage. Vernon and Sally tried to mediate as the four of us poured forth our emotions for hours. They admonished Helen and me, saying we were being very selfish and showing little or no concern for our children. I decided to ignore my own feelings and wait for Helen to give evidence she wanted me to come back.

I continued to attend church, hoping to learn more about this Christianity thing. As fate would have it, I met a Christian girl in the church singles group who wanted to be friends, and perhaps help me though my crisis. We became very good friends, and the more our relationship progressed, the less desire I had to return to Helen.

Florida has "no fault divorce." Helen used the law to file for divorce. I lost when I tried to fight it and had to pay both attorneys and the court costs. My visitation privileges allowed me to have ten-year-old Veronica and nine-year-old Sebastian every weekend.

I lived aboard my boat for three months. The club provided a pool for the kids and I had a food and beverage minimum to meet. When the air conditioning went out on the boat we moved into an apartment in Palmetto.

One weeknight Sebastian appeared at my door. He had ridden his bike over ten miles because he wanted to stay with me. He was sad and disappointed when I told him he couldn't stay. I called Helen and asked, "Where's Sebastian?"

"He's asleep in his room."

"Go look," I said. When she came back to the phone I told her Sebastian was with me and didn't want to leave.

"If that's the way he feels about it, you keep him."

Helen had no contact with Sebastian for months. I kept the support payments going in order to keep the peace.

My "red impulse," so called by my family, was a new, fully loaded, red Trans Am, which I saw and then stopped to buy without thinking. The transaction took about ten minutes; both my salary and my credit rating were quite high.

A friend from the church singles group, (she had a daughter Veronica's age) was pretty, had a good personality, and was an encouraging friend. We spent a lot of time together.

The security my job offered always appeared to be the primary factor with women who were interested in marriage. My mental background seemed of little importance—something from the past. They never wanted to discuss it.

I had already had dinner with my new girl friend's mom and dad, and it looked as though we were headed for marriage, when my "red impulse" struck again.

I met the stepdaughter of another woman who was also in the singles group. One Saturday we spent the day talking and sailing and then she and our four kids spent the night at my apartment: her two kids in one bedroom and my two in the other.

She and I stayed on the couch, but were too busy to sleep much. I proposed marriage in the morning. She agreed. When I told "my intended" on Monday, she looked at me with disbelief. To assuage my guilt, I hired her to join my staff.

I bought a house large enough to house our family of six. Veronica was spending more and more time with me, because all four of the kids were enrolled in the Community Christian School. When Veronica became difficult for Helen to handle she sent my daughter to live with me. I continued child support payments

My new girl friend seemed quite a good mother. We had our rings made and approached the new pastor of the Baptist Church to arrange our wedding. He gave us a flat no for an answer. He did not marry divorced people—no exceptions. So we planned a future trip to the courthouse.

Three months later, before we actually married, the honeymoon ended with a catastrophic emotional battle. She revealed her ability to scream and yell uncontrollably. My hypo manic, dogmatic attitude wouldn't allow me to understand. We parted.

Nineteen – A New Wife

When a man opens the car door for his wife,
it's either a new car or a new wife.
Prince Philip

I returned to my earlier girl friend and began seeing her outside of work. She asked a friend of hers who lived a few blocks from me if she would consider inviting me and the children for a home-cooked dinner. The invitation from Bonnie came several evenings later.

After dinner the "red impulse" struck again, and I asked Bonnie if she would marry me. She laughed, a bit uncomfortable, but didn't reply. Three months later a different pastor from a different church married us.

Her son was Sebastian's age. Veronica stayed with us now, so we had a great family of five. I continued to pay child support to keep Helen happy, but Bonnie thought it very unfair; she wasn't receiving support from her ex-husband. She was right, of course.

When I called Helen and told her I wouldn't be paying any more child support, she threatened to come get the kids.

I dreaded hearing this, but Bonnie picked up the phone and called an attorney she knew well, who had been a judge and state senator. Within an hour we were in his office. When he learned the facts of the situation he called Helen's attorney. An agreement was reached immediately and his legal assistant drew up the papers awarding me permanent custody.

The next morning Helen called me at my office, ending our conversation with, "and by the way, your dad *did* blame you for your mother's death."

A notary took the papers to her house that afternoon and the next day I picked up the official "Judges Motion of Permanent Custody to the father of the minor children, Veronica Lee Patton and Sebastian Bernard Patton."

For the next four years, from 1981 to 1985, we had a normal family life. I learned to recognize my minor emotional swings and listen to my mind telling me to conduct myself properly. We attended a charismatic church—Pentecostal, or Holy Roller. The sermons were almost entirely based on emotion, but we all enjoyed the music and the performance. I learned very little about the faith. Bonnie and I actually taught Sunday school to the mid-high group. I decided to reread the Bible and continued to do so, although I was very confused.

Every day at breakfast, we read devotionals. Sometimes I played my guitar and we sang together. I thought my family and I were on our way to becoming good Christians.

Often missionaries came to church on Sundays to speak of their experiences in foreign lands. I envisioned these adventurous folks as selfless and mercy-minded—without the comforts of home, family and friends. They told of riding a mule through the jungle, wearing pith helmets and carrying a Bible. I admired them. I was no preacher; I hardly understood my faith.

In January 1985, the middle-high school group of kids planned a short-term mission to Haiti. Four youth pastors from other churches were going in advance to scout for projects that could be undertaken by their groups. I was asked to join them as a lay youth pastor. We spent a week in Haiti coordinating different tasks that could be accomplished by small groups.

I met Will at the Baptist Haiti Mission, which was, by far, the largest and most active mission in the country. They had 220 churches, 185 schools, and an extensive agro-forestry project. In addition, the mission ran a two-hundred-bed hospital and tuberculosis sanitarium, a support program for orphans and schoolchildren and had a million-dollar-per-year donor base. We talked at length about his need for a microcomputer network programmer and analyst for his mission. He looked at me and said, "You need to come down. We have living quarters for you and your family."

This assignment didn't require a mule, pith helmet, or Bible, but it was something I could do and do well. I hadn't imagined high-tech had made inroads even as far as this God-forsaken country. The opportunity excited me and when I told the men who were with me, they were especially encouraging.

We had made our base in a cabin in the mountains over six thousand feet above Port-au-Prince. At that altitude it could become very cold in spite of the tropical heat that covered the few lowlands in the country. We put our fireplace to good use.

The peasants were in the midst of Carnival, or Mardi Gras, season, which begins on or after epiphany and ends on the day before Ash Wednesday. Roman Catholic traditions in Haiti drastically changed over the centuries. The influence of polytheism and Voodoo's animism resulted in a spiritualistic Catholic faith dominating the culture. The claim that Haiti was eighty-per-cent Catholic and a hundred-per-cent Voodoo was well accepted. I would visit ceremonies and learn more in years to come, but at the time had no idea what was really going on.

Just below our cabin, drums beat all night, accompanied by blood-curdling screams, large fires, dancing and indistinguishable shouts. These Rah-Rahs, or Fets, were ongoing countrywide. One by one, we drifted off to our small rooms to sleep for the night: we had some long-distance traveling to do the next day.

I slipped off to sleep trying to interpret the rhythm of the drums below.

Two hours later, I woke to the same sounds. I got up and walked to the fireplace. The flames had died out but the fire sill smoldered.

When I returned to my room I encountered an otherworldly darkness, blacker than black—like a curtain barring my entrance. Suddenly I felt extremely cold and experienced a fear unlike any I had ever known before.

My terror increased as a large grotesque image of a face took shape—morphing itself as though to become clearer. I waited for my mind to grasp its full gaze.

I have had vivid dreams, occult experiences, hallucinations, and psychotic delusions. This time I had all my wits about me: I was not even hypomanic. This apparition seemed as real as my own hand, which I brought up to shield my eyes as the image solidified.

For the first time in my life, I involuntary shouted, "In the name of Jesus, get away from me." Immediately I found myself next to my empty bed in the dim light that came from the outer room.

I heard my New Zealander, evangelist friend call out. "You alright Rich?" I assured him I was. He was the charismatic one of the group and a world-traveled evangelist. His voice seemed reassuring.

I was convinced I had a glimpse into the transcendental netherworld of ultimate evil itself. My ontological convictions had taken a great leap forward. Indeed, I had been visited by an angel, an evil one to be sure, but an angel nonetheless. In Haiti evil shows itself clearly; back home it is often very subtle. You can join or fight against it—would that my angel had been a holy one.

Having coordinated the summer projects for some short-term missions, we flew back to Tampa.

Twenty – Career Move to Haiti

But Satan now is wiser than of yore, and tempts
by making rich, not making poor.
Alexander Pope

On the way home from the airport, Bonnie and I stopped at a restaurant. I told her I was considering moving our family to Haiti, initially for a one-year commitment, with subsequent consideration for an indefinite stay.

Bonnie and the three kids would benefit from exposure to the extreme cultural differences and we could all find some way to serve. Bonnie felt at peace about this move after receiving support from her many friends in the church. The elders and pastors knew of my illness and said I should consider the effects the move might have on me, seek God in the decision, and wait before confirming my plans.

I would be resigning from a very secure career with high salary and benefits that would make my family secure for life and guarantee a college education for all of my three children.

I sat in my home office about 4:00 a.m., as had become my habit, to read the Bible and pray. Since my conversion, emotional as it was, my hypomania had directed me to become a spiritual individual. I would later admit I had the habit of finding examples and interpreting them to coincide with what I wanted to hear.

One day I heard a man seeking direction, not unlike myself, randomly turned to a verse in his Bible: "and Judas went out and hanged himself." Not satisfied, he selected randomly again, closed his eyes, and pointed to the verse "go thou and do likewise." Very frustrated, he closed his Bible, opened it again and in that same manner found the verse "what thou doest, do quickly."

But in my current state, I found the verse, "For I know the thoughts that I think toward you, saith the LORD, thoughts of peace, and not of evil, to give you an expected end." My sister agreed with my interpretation and encouraged me to make the move.

I immediately typed out my resignation letter with a two-week notice and hoped it would be accepted. They released me from my contract and I continued moonlighting work with various clients until we departed for Haiti three months later.

I took a seven-day water-only fast to see if God would speak to my mind and offer some form of confirmation. In the end, all I heard, as I lay prostrate was "get up and fix yourself some scrambled eggs." I suppose He knew my mind was already made up, so the immediate need was to end the fast and not get sick.

A Haitian friend gave us some initial lessons in the French Creole language, we found someone to rent our house, and the school board released me with a big going away party. They made me promise to come back in July to finish a major project for the State Department of Education.

In mid-April of '85, we were driven to Ft. Lauderdale and stayed one night in very modest mission housing. The next morning Bonnie, Veronica, sixteen, Sebastian and Matthew, fifteen, and I flew to Port-au-Prince, Haiti aboard a 1938 war-torn DC3 restored for Missionary Flights International. I had my illness under control. Or so I thought.

Getting through customs was worse than my previous visit. I had warned everyone to expect the machine gun-carrying guards, the Tonton Macoutes, and the arrogant attitude of the custom officials. I found out later it just took a little money to get through quickly.

The Tonton Macoutes, a Haitian paramilitary force created in 1959, reported directly to François "Papa Doc" Duvalier and after his death in 1971, to his son, Jean-Claude. The younger Duvalier was ousted in a rebellion February 1986 only ten months after we arrived.

The name Tonton Macoute (translates as "Uncle Gunnysack") originated from Haitian Creole mythology. It was the name of a bogeyman that walked the streets after dark and kidnapped children who stayed out too late. He stowed them away in his gunnysack and they were never seen again.

Duvalier employed the Tonton Macoutes in a reign of terror against any opponents, including those who proposed progressive social systems. Those who spoke out against Duvalier were sometimes attacked in broad daylight or disappeared during the night, never to be found. They were believed to have been abducted and killed by the MVSN, (Militia Volontaires de la Sécurité Nationale) who were therefore known as the Tonton Macoutes. Since they reported directly to the dictator, anyone who challenged the MVSN risked assassination. Their unrestrained terrorism was accompanied by corruption, extortion and personal aggrandizement among the leadership.

In '86 the new government disbanded the MVSN, but some members became insurgents against the new leadership and participated in the ensuing political turmoil, particularly in rural areas, up until 2000.

But this was April 1985. A pickup met us outside the François Duvalier International Airport. It was an hour's drive up thirty-five degree slopes with no guardrail to protect vehicles from running off the road and tumbling thousands of feet below.

It had been hot and humid at the airport and like a demolition derby getting through Port-au-Prince. But it was cool and dry at over 6,400 feet in the small village of Femathe, where the main mission compound was located.

Several Haitians had been in the truck to unload all our family items into the small three-bed room apartment. From the living room windows we could look down the thousand-foot drop to the valley below and up at the even larger mountains on the other side, far south of Port-au-Prince. The view was breathtaking. Clouds arrived through our windows frequently—brief travelers bringing an extra chill. We had one bathroom and a kitchen served by the rain on the roof, draining to a cistern below. Showers were ice-cold and the water had to be filtered for cooking, and drinking.

The Church of the Cross guaranteed us a monthly salary of four hundred dollars and a number of our supporters among the membership graciously added about seven hundred each month, although those contributions diminished significantly over time. The apartment was free and a maid was provided at 175 gourdes a month, or thirty-five dollars. We were told having a maid was necessary, as Bonnie, being a white woman, would be charged four or five times more when she shopped at the markets. The average annual salary for Haitians was only the equivalent of a hundred U.S. dollars, so hiring Marie was a benefit for her as well as for us. She remained with us even when we moved to another location and years later named her second female child after Bonnie.

I started work with Will, the son of Pastor William, once we were settled and Bonnie had the kids started on their home-school studies. The curriculum was designed mostly for self-study with some assistance from parents, except when taking tests. The mail went out once a week on the MFI DC3 and graded assignments were returned a week later.

The A Beka curriculum from Pensacola Christian School proved too much for our kids who were used to a classroom setting, so Will agreed to pay for their tuition to Quisqueya Christian School down in PaP, a missionary and business dependents' school. There, the many English-speaking classmates became close friends with Matthew, Sebastian and Veronica.

After having coded several applications during the first seven months, my work at the mission became one of network maintenance. I had time to return to Florida and finish the project for the School Board. I began helping other missions by setting up their systems for them from my own customizable accounting package. I worked for whatever donations they offered.

Using the resources of BHM (Baptist Haiti Mission), I also led short-term mission groups from the U.S. and Canada. The projects were located at many worksites all over Haiti, but mostly in the provinces outside of Port-au-Prince. It was obvious these teens and adults alike were very affected by these one or two week trips. They may have done something for the Haitians, but the hearts of the volunteers were changed. The mission turned out to be more beneficial for the foreign team missionaries than the Haitians themselves.

By December, my work at BHM was concluded. The Haiti office of Compassion International was its largest foreign-based operation that served over 1.2 million children in twenty-six countries. Derek, the Field Director, was a good friend. He knew of my former career in education and asked me to apply for the job of Director of Education.

He found a home for us in the mountains forty-five hundred feet above Port-au-Prince. Wealthy Haitians who had fled the Duvalier regime and now lived in New York owned the property. This five-level home had a ten-foot high moss-covered stone fence surrounding a 100x300 foot yard garden, terraced down a forty-degree slope. We could see mountains in the Dominican Republic and the salt lake in the middle of the two countries.

The owners accepted the offer of four hundred U.S. dollars a month; we had to keep and pay the yard-boy, Joseph. They were just happy to have some Americans living in and keeping up their house. We moved in, taking Marie with us.

Two weeks before Christmas, Bonnie and I flew Missionary Flights International to Ft. Lauderdale where we made a commercial connection to Compassion's corporate office in Colorado Springs to be interviewed for the new position. We gave the MFI pilot some cash to buy McDonald's meals for our three children when he picked them up on his next week's flight to Florida, where we would meet them. We had left them in Haiti with a missionary family whose children they knew, so the kids could finish the semester at Quisqueya.

After three days of psychological, language and aptitude tests, and a score of interviews, they realized we were both divorced and remarried. Bonnie and I would be perfect for the job, but they were sorry. Instead I was to be the Acting Country Field Director whenever Derek was out of country, which was fairly frequent. Some of the many different denominational leaders Compassion deals with would be offended if the Director of Education had been divorced.

Twenty-one – Spiral Downward

*The world is a Dangerous place to live; not because of the people who are
evil, but because of the people who don't do anything about it.*
Albert Einstein

Disappointed but still undaunted, I decided to increase my client
base, keep the home in Laboule, and see what happened. I really
loved Haiti; our life there could fill an entire book.

We flew back to Tampa, found a ride home to Bradenton, and David
loaned us a hopped-up Mustang to drive while we were in the States.
Bonnie and I began our Christmas visiting and four days later returned to
Ft. Lauderdale to meet the MFI plane to pick up the kids and drive back
to Bradenton for the holidays.

I spoke about our work and plans in Haiti to the two services at church.
At David's request they took up an offering for us to buy a vehicle—we had
been using BHM Jeeps. We stayed with Bonnie's mom until we returned
to Haiti immediately after the New Year.

Within six months, I was serving as many as twenty-two clients
across Haiti. For most clients I set up and customized my accounting
systems for DOS, UNIX and Novell Netware. United States Agency
for International Development required me to customize a standard
accounting system for all their projects, as well as establish defined and
measurable empirical data collection for statistical analysis and annual

evaluation. These projects varied from agro forestry to medical records, and from water shed management to farming methods—including the cloning of pineapple tops.

Bonnie began to work with an American woman once we bought a second car. After I set up an accounts receivable system for Bonnie to use at Minnie's office, all data was inputted from paper files. They discovered she had $320,000 in receivables.

Minnie had studied Bavarian Folk Art in Switzerland. Here she had great success teaching twenty-five or so Haitians to buy fifty-gallon drums and chisel out the lids and bottoms. She had another thirty workers chisel designs out of the steel and paint them for gifts. Her cost for the various works of art was about ten dollars: she signed and sold them to gift shops worldwide for eighty-five to one-hundred dollars apiece.

Apparently Sebastian had been going through a crisis for some time. He had been the one I thought would want to stay, but he ran away to the US Embassy to try to leave. When they called, I knew it was time to let him go home. At the end of January, just before the uprising, I arranged for him to live with the Pastor from our church and reluctantly sent him home.

A few days later, I was in the bedroom he left and thumbed through the Bible he had asked for the prior Christmas. I came across a three-by-five inch card. It read, "Satan, if you get me out of here, I'll serve you for ten years." This was extremely disturbing: Sebastian had shown evidence of a Christian belief since he was eight years old. We belonged to a charismatic church and the worst thing according to their theology was the role that Satan played in the destruction of a soul. Sebastian knew this and must have had a similar belief. He had no expectation that I would find his plea. I feel certain he had appealed to God at first, but to no avail. I kept this to myself for years as I watched Sebastian develop first into a spiritual apostasy and finally to disbelief altogether. I still have a somewhat open dialog with him about this.

February 6, 1986 Jean Claude Duvalier, the dictator, was forced out of the country. The average Haitian turned against the corrupt police, forty-five thousand Tonton Macoutes, and seven thousand military. We had to stay away from the windows for three days as peasants killed and stole weapons from these corrupt former official government personnel. The peasants were very dangerous with these automatic weapons, primarily from lack of experience and decades of anger.

A new Haitian Creole word was introduced: "deshukay." It meant to utterly destroy each large home that could be found. Hundreds of peasants at a time joined to remove everything in the house, from paintings, to toilets to light fixtures. Everything.

The mobs came closer to our home and finally reached the houses on either side of us. When Joseph, our yard-boy, assured the rebels we were Americans, not corrupt government officials, they left us alone. Even so, being surrounded by four hundred Haitians who were wreaking homes, taking booty, and randomly firing in every direction was a terrifying experience. Down in Port-au-Prince the mobs were castrating their enemies, burning them to death or beheading them. We were fortunate to see this only second hand in photographs. For the whites, business and travel stopped for a week or so before returning to normal, but it was many months later for mulattos.

For the duration of our residence in Haiti, we adapted to the culture and continued to be a regular American family to the extent possible: Kids in school, mom and dad working, much as it would be in the States. Every day was exciting and challenging. I was never bored.

By summer of 1987, a few months more than two years after our move, I felt myself slipping into a depression. I had heard of Elavil, so I bought sixty tablets at a pharmacy where whites could buy anything without prescription. The generic drug, amitriptyline, is a tricyclic antidepressant and I was not aware that mania was a possible side effect. I felt a change the very next morning as soon as I awakened. By the end of the week, I was almost fully manic. I became completely controlled by the idea that I had to get out of Haiti at least for a time. My discussions with Bonnie were furious and one-sided. Any time she questioned why I wanted to leave, I went into a diatribe concerning my leadership of the family. On a sort of automatic pilot, I filed for our exit visas, paid off the officials to obtain them, and bought plane tickets for Bonnie and me to return to Florida. I do not recall my reasoning: I was likely operating on emotions that were out of my control.

Bonnie had never seen me in a manic state. When we reached Bradenton she used Florida's Baker Act, which authorizes involuntary hospitalization, to get me admitted to the psychiatric hospital. I stayed only the mandatory seventy-two hours. Even though she knew my history, this personal experience was too shocking for her. She seemed to give up on me, so she returned to Haiti and had a garage sale for missionaries from the International Fellowship. She brought back the little that remained, along with Veronica and Matthew, on Agape' Flights out of Sarasota. We moved back into our house in Bradenton

Veronica graduated from high school and joined Youth With A Mission in Cambridge, Ontario, Canada. Later she did extended cross-cultural evangelism with YWAM in South and Central America. Matthew attended his senior year at Manatee High. Sebastian, still underage, wanted to marry Sheila, a sweet and lovely girl. At the time, I was hospitalized once again: he had to come to me for my written permission.

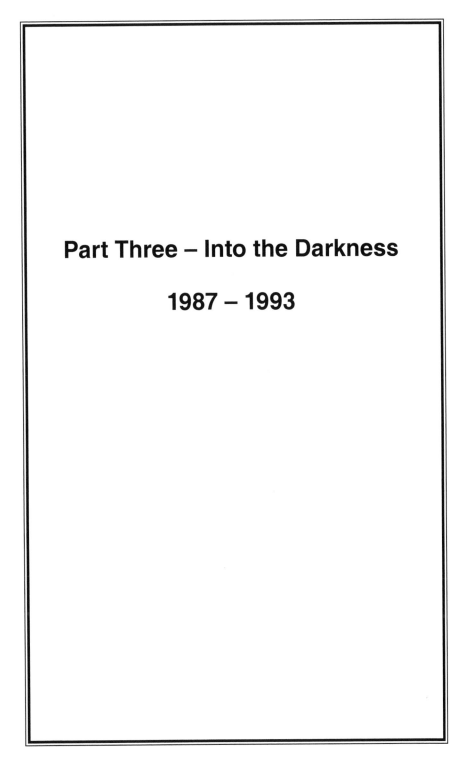

Part Three – Into the Darkness

1987 – 1993

Twenty-two – Send the Marines

So when in doubt, send the Marines.
Tom Lehrer

My income was a fraction of what it had been when Bonnie and I first married and I worked for the school board. Bonnie missed the security and couldn't deal with my manic depression. When Veronica returned from her eight months service with YWAM, Bonnie told me to leave, but that Veronica could stay with her. When my daughter said she wanted to live with me, I quickly found an apartment for the two of us.

After a quick uncontested divorce, I continued to serve in Haiti by commuting for two or three-week stays. My clients paid well and all my expenses were covered. Some USAID project administrators even traveled to Florida for my help. But over a year's time the work dwindled.

I made one last three-week trip to Haiti to conclude my findings for Associates in Rural Development. The compound was located in the far southwest tip of Haiti in a village named Camp Perrin, one-hundred-forty miles from Port-au-Prince. I drank eight or ten martinis on the plane and was hypomanic when I arrived. The project director picked me up at the airport and took me directly to the site.

I worked hard for three weeks, slowly progressing into a full manic state. Just before trying to leave I learned a good friend of mine—a horticulturist who was married—and a female PhD had their own "fatal attraction." He told his wife of the affair, but the other woman refused to leave him alone.

A Haitian manservant told me about a trick appropriate to this situation. So I placed a dead tarantula, a generous supply of blood from my own sliced finger, and a travel agents card from PaP, into a box. The Haitian said he would take it to "the other woman" at midnight after he found a hougan, or Vodou priest, to bless it.

The woman did not show up for work at the compound the next day. The administrator had been in on the trick so he went to her hut around noon. He found her extremely ill and wanting to go home—go figure. I think it is a psycho-spiritual fear that engulfs some people.

My own mania seemed to shift in and out of a psychotic state. My emotional reasoning took over my brain, telling me to leave immediately for Port-au-Prince on foot. It was about sundown.

Creole was becoming my primary language. Normally, I was not very fluent, but in my state, I was actually thinking in Creole. A white man walking the road was almost never seen and cars and jeeps didn't travel at more than 15mph. (The weekend this narrow highway out of Les Cayes was opened a few years before, almost a hundred Haitians were hit and killed.) There was little traffic on the road, but I was given short rides by most who passed by. How I ended up in Jacmel, I'll never know; it was on a different road south, forty miles from PaP, over a series of seven-to-nine-thousand foot mountain ranges.

I ran into a couple of mulatto Haitians who wanted to party at the beautiful hotel overlooking the Caribbean. We were only one of a few groups staying at the hotel. The next thing I knew, I was in a car with a group of young missionaries who took me to Steve's in Pe'tionville just north of PaP. I had met Steve early on when I worked for him at Pan American Development Foundation. He had been in Haiti twenty-five years. Steve told me ARD had called him when I disappeared. It had taken me a week to reach Jacmel.

Steve knew I was dangerous: he'd experienced a less intense version of my illness before and with my refusal to speak English, I would be a target for the military or police at the Port-au-Prince airport. He arranged for two US Embassy Marine guards to travel with the two of us to the newly named PaP International Airport, then on to Miami.

With no passport or exit visa, I was lugged arm-in-arm by the two Marines directly to a commercial aircraft. They stuffed me in a seat between them on the plane, and gave me all the drinks I could handle to keep me quiet. It was a good thing the marines didn't know French Creole: in lucid moments between drinks I disrespected them and their mothers to the amusement and fear of the other, mostly Haitian, passengers. I passed out several times from the alcohol medication.

In Miami, they dragged me straight through the airport, bypassing immigration and customs through forbidden doors—directly to where my sister had been given permission to park. Steve told me to get in the back; he got in the front passenger's seat.

Patty had driven my car to meet us and drive us back to Bradenton—a three-hundred mile round trip. It was an hour-and-a-half drive to Lake Okeechobee and another one-hundred fifty miles farther to reach home. By the time we were halfway to the lake, where we turned northwest, I had assimilated all the alcohol. I lost consciousness in the brain sense and became psychotic. I learned later I had reached forward and tried to put the gears in reverse. They stopped the car and I jumped out into the other lane, almost causing a semi-truck to jackknife. It took the strength of both of them to wrestle me back into the car. Looking at the map they found the only nearby town of any size. Steve and Patty were directed by the police to a small crisis-stabilization facility.

In a small room I thrashed and screamed in Creole, while at least five people strapped down my hands and feet. For two thirty-minute periods they tested my resistance. I was told later it took three large shots of Thorazine to finally knock me out. I had gone without sleep for eleven days.

I awakened days later with the old familiar anxiety and depression coming from my foggy brain. I could now articulate in English. I stayed in the facility for another week until Patty was certain she would have no trouble picking me up for the return to the hospital in Bradenton.

After three or four weeks I was released, just happy to get out of there. I was feeling somewhat normal, but lacking motivation and confidence. Getting back to work was difficult.

Twenty-three – Armed and Dangerous

Take time to deliberate, but when the time for action has arrived,
stop thinking and go in.
Napoleon Bonaparte

Two of my stateside clients were a County Administration and a Sheriff's Department. I coded several systems for them from Fleet Maintenance to Physical Plant Services and got to know most of the brass, all of whom were very friendly.

It was early 1989 and I had the crazy idea I wanted to carry a firearm because I traveled to some strange places. I asked some deputies in the Sheriff's Department about getting a permit and they casually said, "Go ahead and get what you want. It just has to be hidden. Do not pull it out unless you plan to kill someone. We will take care of the paper work for you."

I bought a first class .38 cal revolver, an ankle holster and a box of rounds. I couldn't wait to get it loaded and strapped on. The fear I had experienced encountering Nicaraguan rebels, witnessing Haitian riots, and even stopping at 7-Elevens in bad parts of town drifted away; I felt like James Bond.

At the time, I was servicing five clients in the Tampa Bay area and five clients out of the country. I had been hypomanic for months, which allowed me to efficiently cover my workload. As long as I had some sleep, I could preserve this emotional state without becoming manic or worse.

A few months after purchasing the gun, my nephew, Ben, and I boarded my sailboat for a three-day sail from St. Petersburg, under the Skyway Bridge, to Egmont Key and Bahia Beach. Sailing almost always relaxed me from my hypomania.

While still inside the Intracoastal Waterway, we were enjoying some good classical music on the Ghetto Blaster. It was comfortably perched on the cabin top when some jackass in a speedboat passed on the starboard side at full throttle and very close. The music disappeared along with the boom box into fifteen feet of water.

My instant response was to pull out my weapon and fire all six shots at the rapidly vanishing boatload of people. My mind probably gave the okay, knowing I couldn't hit anything farther than ten feet away. On the other hand, perhaps this was a case of emotional reasoning.

I reloaded and holstered my pistol in case the boat turned to come back. Apparently they never heard the shot above the sound of their large engine. I was lucky they weren't headed for the hospital. Ben just laughed; nothing I did surprised him, and still doesn't. We had fired several types of weapons together before, in an unorthodox and rather dangerous manner.

I let Ben drink only beer, as his mother had allowed me the same privilege at the same age. I continued to drink from my stash of gallon bottles of cheap Bali Hai wine, hoping it would make me sleep at night and avoid a manic episode. We reached the Key in the darkness, dropped the hook and hit the sack. It had been a long sail, twenty-six nautical miles in light air, over around nine hours.

We ended up on the windward side of the island, where the wind picked up and tossed the boat most of the night. Ben passed on breakfast, saying he felt nauseous. From experience, I knew how to cure what ailed him.

I gave Ben a can of beer and a small towel in an airtight baggie and told him to swim to shore, sit on the beach, and sip the beer. He protested, but did as I said. We were only fifty yards from shore, but the Gulf water temperature in January is usually in the mid-fifties. I could hear his teeth chattering until he reached the beach.

I've had some people refuse to come back—they would rather stay on this deserted island—so I always plan to swim over myself to encourage them to return to the boat. Ben looked so lonesome, huddled by some sea oats sipping his beer. It reminded me of my first, and only snipe hunt when I was ten. I dove in and swam quickly, telling myself I was right: the temperature of the water had to be less than sixty degrees.

Ben said it was no fun but he did feel much better and warmer. We waited a while and just talked. I told him about flying low over Egmont Key seeing scores of sharks swimming about the southern tip, where we were now. I assured him that it takes a shark quite a while to assess something as large as a fast human swimmer before attacking.

"The ladder is down off the stern, I have the oven heating the cabin and you have both hands to swim with this time," I encouraged him.

"Can't you bring the boat closer?"

"No, gets too shallow somewhere in between."

"Why don't you have a dinghy anyway?"

"Slows the boat down."

"Whoa man!"

"Race ya back," I said as I dove in.

He was at the boat in gold-medal free-style time; it seemed less than a minute. I only learned to swim distances with the slow sidestroke; Ben was there before I made two-thirds of the distance. He was grinning ear to ear; a good character building exercise.

While Ben had some breakfast and coffee, I set sail for Bahia Beach. I felt great too. The winds were from the NE about fifteen knots. The direct course was nineteen nautical miles on a northeasterly course. This time some tacking was required, making the trip closer to 26nm in five tacks, and about six hours.

When we reached our destination, Ben went to the heated swimming pool before we grilled our own steaks at the dock, and then my crewman went to bed early. To assure some sleep, I went to the bar for some alcohol to medicate myself.

I was accustomed to drinking wine, so I miscalculated my dosage: the double-bourbons were a bit of an overdose. I blacked out and remembered nothing until late the next morning. Ben was nowhere to be found.

After searching for some time, I called my sister. Apparently, during the night I went into some kind of rage that scared Ben enough to call his mom and ask to be picked up. He did not relate all the details to my sister, but months later he did tell me his perception of the episode.

Although I have no recollection of sailing back to St. Petersburg, I must have done so without event. I guess sailing can be a subconscious endeavor, given my years of experience—just like driving a car. I had sailed all day and well into the night.

Twenty-four – Felony

I became insane, with long intervals of horrible sanity.
Edgar Allan Poe

A day or two later I went to work on-site at one of my long-standing clients. As doctors, they were aware of my illness and its difficulties, but they valued my work highly and overlooked my mood swings.

While sitting and conversing with the main office manager, someone knocked on the door. When it opened, I saw a County Deputy Sheriff. He asked if he could speak to me outside. I followed thinking maybe it was a message from the Sheriff, requesting some work of the same nature as that of the Sarasota Sheriff.

The cars and six deputies were waiting with pistols in hand and told me to hit the ground with my hands behind my back. As they attempted to take my firearm and cuff me, my mind sped back to all the other times I had been cuffed and forced into the cramped back seat of a cop car. At that moment I lost consciousness and did not come back for days.

Apparently I didn't pass out. I stood up and began to fight all six deputies. Patients, doctors, and employees all witnessed this debacle through the plate-glass window. I was later told I got in a number of punches and kicks until they drew their batons and literally beat me to a pulp. They could have checked with my client's sheriff to the south, but they were dealing with an insane armed suspect; their actions were understandable. I was charged with a felony and sent off to jail: an illegal concealed firearm without a permit, assaulting law officers, and resisting arrest. I never found out who told them of my pistol.

When I again became aware of my existence, I discovered I was lying on cement looking up at cement. My arm and shoulder were covered in some viscous substance. It looked like mud, but under closer examination, I recognized a mixture of various foods, my excrement, and urine—and I was lying in it, too. Aluminum trays littered the room. As I sat up, I found I was naked. These discoveries came slowly but I definitely knew they were real.

A man was steering a ship in the corner. He turned and shouted some orders to me I could not understand, and as he faced me I knew who it was: Adolf Hitler. In the other corner, Faye Dunaway lay dead. Then a wrecking ball came crashing through the wall behind me and outside light flowed in. Really! But not actually; instead, hallucinations, and bizarre synapses.

I stood. Faye, Adolph and the wrecking ball dissolved; a jail cell slowly emerged to be my true surroundings. Visual and auditory phantasms had long since become a source of detached curiosity to some degree—like watching a horror movie. They continued to change and evolve, but they always went away eventually. I have heartfelt sympathy for the schizophrenics.

Aside from the "mud pies," I felt a great deal of pain all over my body. I was covered with scores of rancid boils and had no idea they came from the baton strikes. My unsanitary environment had exacerbated them. I did not know how long I had been in this place.

I wandered around in the cell until the hallucinations ceased and my perception of the surroundings began to make sense. A huge black man stepped within four feet of my cell door and commanded me to step to the back of the cell. After I judged him real, I did as he said. He quickly moved forward and placed a tray in the door of my cell then disappeared in a half-second. I hungrily ate the breakfast without thinking even for a minute of adding it to the mud-pies. From the sheer magnitude of the mess, I must have been throwing meal trays for days.

Across from my cell was another cell-like structure housing two deputies. I had been under observation all along. As I looked, one of them "gave me the finger," and the other yelled something accompanied by a different lewd gesture. I could not hear him but he had an angry expression on his face. The cubicle they were in was made of glass. I had the idea they were testing my attitude and I did not return their gestures in kind. When one held up a nude centerfold of a pretty girl, I just smiled. These little tests must have triggered what happened next.

Four large deputies, with batons in hand, appeared at the cell door and told me to step back. They were all business and warned me of the consequence of not following and doing exactly as they ordered.

They circled my nude, dirty body. I moved down the hall as directed, accompanied by complaints toward my person, my mother's character, my lack of intelligence, and so on. With rubber-gloved hands, they all but carried me.

We reached a small cement alcove and I was shoved inside. While three remained in a menacing stance ready to strike me, the other produced a water hose that felt like a fire truck was behind it. They told me to turn repeatedly. Serious at first, they were now having a great time assaulting me verbally and with the stinging water.

After fifteen minutes the torrent of water stopped and they tossed me a towel. Much more kindly and professionally, they asked if I felt better. I did. They returned me to a different cell, with all white bars and walls. I was in the hospital section.

I received no medication, but ten days later I was transferred to the psychiatric facility. They released me two weeks later—with new meds. With the help of my sister's efforts with the State's attorney, and my records of mental illness, the charges were dismissed.

A felony arrest or any other arrest stays on your record regardless of your guilt or innocence. If prospective employers do a background search, they see Felony Illegal Weapon, Firearm. They generally do not look further into the record to learn of one's innocence. The fifteen arrests in my juvenile record had long since been expunged. I was now starting a record that would follow me everywhere.

Twenty-five – Stripper and the Swat Team

Lust's passion will be served; it demands, it militates, it tyrannizes.
Marquis de Sade

I was weary of troubling my family and decided to leave. Ben drove me to the north end of the Skyway Bridge leading to St. Petersburg, forty-five miles from my home in Bradenton. When we stopped he handed me a small ash stick hanging from a leather loop. The State had taken away my right to carry a firearm, so my nephew's fish bat would have to serve as protection for now.

There was genuine concern on his face as I told him not to follow me or tell anyone one in the family where he had last seen me. I made my way by city bus, lugging my clothes and few belongings in a small duffle bag to St. Petersburg's downtown area. I rented a room in the rundown, drug-infested neighborhood northeast of William's Park. My primary hypomanic plan was to find a job and stay apart from my family until I had done so.

I was still not sleeping, taking no medication, and avoiding alcohol. I spent my nights at the shabby twenty-four-hour diner on Fourth Street called "Ham and Eggs." There were several live-in facilities for mental patients and drug rehab surrounding the diner. My small crack hole was only three blocks away. Between midnight and dawn at the diner, I met many people like me from the surrounding slums. I even ran into a friend from high school—we'd had a knockdown, drag-out fight twenty-two years before. I broke my hand on his head and he broke my nose for the second time since summer camp. We reminisced; he was schizophrenic and lived in a free facility nearby.

Dressed neatly and carrying a Nikon camera around my neck, I stood out a bit from the rest. Early one morning I met a young girl. "You should come see me dance," she said. She was obviously a runaway.

I was quickly approaching a manic state and became quite indignant about her situation as she told me her story of drugs and sexual abuse. Although inappropriate, the emotional part of me responded sexually. When I asked to see some ID, she produced a dilapidated driver's license from Wisconsin. The DOB checked out; she was eighteen by five months and indeed, a runaway. From my point of view the picture on her license looked like a young child. However, the girl sitting across from me was a beautiful young woman; her name was Marcy. She seemed pleased to have someone concerned for her.

The next afternoon, I visited the nude "gentlemen's" club and watched while five or six girls "strutted their stuff." When Marcy came on, my mania-induced lust was the strongest I had ever experienced. I'd possessed many women; this one possessed me. Near the end of her act, she noticed me and quickly retreated behind the back curtain as if suddenly ashamed.

She returned shortly, dressed, and asked to sit at my table and talk to me. I persuaded her to agree to meet me in the diner in the morning after she got off work and told her I would get tickets for us to return to Wisconsin. When she failed to show up, a plan emerged from my insanity. I went to Maas Brothers, the local department store, and selected a half-carat tiara diamond ring for fifteen-hundred dollars. Showing my passport, driver license, and U.S.A.I.D. identifications convinced the clerk to let me pay for it with a check on a closed account—another felony if caught. I dressed well and made off for the strip club, but she wasn't there. Many of the girls gathered around the bar to look at the ring—and see the idiot that bought it for Marcy. I left the ring with the barmaid and told her she could wear it or pawn it; I included the appraisal sheet.

One of the girls told me Marcy was in Sarasota with Joe and that she was more-or-less his woman, in a slave-type relationship. Joe was in his late forties; I was thirty-seven. In my perverted thinking, I felt within my rights to rescue her.

So I set my briefcase on the bar, told the girls there was a bomb in it and insisted they contact Marcy immediately. Panicked, they protested and said they really did not know exactly where she was in Sarasota. I told them they had fifteen minutes before the bomb would go off—and kill us all.

I sat down at a table off to the side. As I imagined the bomb going off, it became a reality in my thinking. I was never more calm or more assured. Several of the girls came to try to talk me into leaving, but I stayed put.

In a relatively short time, I noticed several men enter the dark room from the front door—with rifles pointing threateningly. The barmaid directed two plain-clothes cops to my table, where they aimed pistols at my head and told me to stand. They searched me for weapons. I sat back down. The small swat team went to the bar to pick up my briefcase and carefully bring it to my table. I remained calm as they questioned me. As my previously induced reality vanished, a mental picture of the actual contents of my briefcase reappeared. No, it is not a bomb, I assured them. "Open it slowly," they demanded.

They went through everything: proper passport, memos and ID from the United States Agency for International Development, U.S. State Department directives and a large DynaTAC 1989 cell phone, conspicuously labeled with "Property of the United States Government." All in a seven-hundred dollar briefcase.

Probably not wishing to do all the complicated paperwork and further investigation, the detective finally said, "We don't know who you are, asshole, but you take your shit and get the hell out of here and don't come back."

The vast majority of these girls, although nude and beautiful, had horrible stories of past incest, abuse and numerous sexual encounters. They fawned over patrons, performed lap dances, where they could touch *you* all over, but reciprocation wasn't allowed. I needed another wife.

While walking the sixteen blocks back to my tiny hovel, I began to lose it. The close encounter with the police probably resulted in my sudden and extreme paranoia. As I lay in the comfort and security of my bed, darkness fell and the paranoia became worse. I had pawned my thousand-dollar camera and lenses for a hundred dollars. Now I was broke and could not buy alcohol or drugs to get me to sleep. By midnight my flesh was crawling and my mind and emotions were in a conflictive race.

I got out of bed with a plan to get myself to the hospital, not to look for help, but to steal some narcotics, sodium pentothal or something similar—anything that would let me sleep. This required a long walk to the hospital through dimly lit streets. I had been born there for God's sake; surely I could find it.

Once I reached the hospital compound I felt better and anticipated a long, sneaking passage through the hospital building. Now the emotional phantasms were in hiding, but all my thoughts were stimulated.

I reached the fourth floor without being seen. I knew they would have drugs in intensive care, but I interrupted my search when I dove into a broom closet to avoid being caught. When I tried again to find a room with drugs, someone else saw me, so I ran back to the broom closet. The sterile smell and quiet of the ward was so peaceful and reassuring that I decided to sleep right there in the closet.

In a manner of minutes, a security guard found me there in a fetal position. I tried to complain of some malady, hoping I would be admitted for treatment, but the guard turned me over to the police. This time I had only my wallet and driver's license with me.

When law enforcement officers arrived, I feared being put in another cell. Only hours before I had been inexplicably lucky in the encounter with the police. How would I fare this time? Once again, the police did not need the extra paperwork an arrest would entail and there was nothing to connect me to the prior event. They questioned me briefly: What is the name of a relative who could take me back to Bradenton? I knew my brother, Currie, attributed all my manic exploits to some lack of character or immaturity, so I chose to give the police the name of my cousin, Richard, who lived only a few miles away.

Richard had joined the service at seventeen and fought the last few months of WWII. Later he served in Korea and did two tours in Viet Nam. He was definitely not afraid of insanity. Richard arrived promptly and took me to his house to get some sleep. I could not, even though I had been awake for almost a week. In the morning, Dick drove me to Bradenton, as he had promised the police, and dropped me off downtown across from the County Courthouse. I was not ready to go home.

For an hour I imposed on a friend from church and owner of a travel service, as he tried to get me a plane ticket to anywhere without credit cards or money. The idea of writing a bad check to him was beyond even my current evil state, so the attempt failed.

I walked a block to the La Vista lounge, sat down and ordered a vodka shot and a draft. When they gave me the tab, I called Sebastian' wife to come get me, and told her I needed a few bucks. She said she would come.

After seven or eight rounds—in a manic state I can consume very large amounts of alcohol without it affecting me—the bartender asked me to pay the tab. I explained someone was coming to pick me up shortly and she would pay the tab, but some jackass at the other end of the bar decided it his duty to force me to pay the bill.

After some name calling, we first shoved each other, and then began to fight. Although he was a head taller and much larger, he was no match for a demon-possessed lunatic. Before the rest of the patrons in the bar pulled me off of him, he was five-times bloodier than I and nearly unconsciousness.

Three was not a charm. Within a twenty-four hour period, I used up all my chances. The cops had only a two-block drive from headquarters. Had I directed my animus to the new arrivals, I knew I would have been charged with assaulting an officer and resisting arrest. I quickly decided to give in, get cuffed, and be stuffed into yet another police car.

Here I was, back in one of the white cells, but with most of my wits about me. The charges were disorderly conduct and defrauding an innkeeper—both second-degree misdemeanors. Mellaril, which is a drug often given unadvisedly for schizophrenia, seems to be the treatment of choice by jail nurses. They weren't privy to my medical record, and probably didn't care. To them, I was behaving like a schizophrenic. They kept me for ten days before releasing me.

Twenty-six – Long Night's Swim

The whole secret of existence is to have no fear. Never fear what will become of you, depend on no one. Only the moment you reject all help are you freed.
Gautama Buddha

Nineteen-eighty-nine was a bad year. I had already been jailed twice, with a felony and two misdemeanors on my arrest record. The time spent in jail, as well as several spells in the psychiatric hospital, caused me to seriously neglect most of my clients. With little money and lots of time I often traveled across the Sunshine Bridge to St. Petersburg, my hometown. Driving around familiar places provided peace to my soul.

On one such occasion, I made my way over to my brother's home in Seminole, an affluent suburb. Arriving at their door without calling first had never been a problem. Currie opened the door and I came in—with my briefcase for some reason. I set my briefcase and keys on the kitchen table and, to my surprise, was questioned angrily by my brother about the contents of my case. Did I have a weapon? I laughed at his seriousness, thinking he must be joking. "That depends on what you mean by a weapon. Look for yourself."

What happened next happened very fast. My comment, and perhaps my appearance, generated an hysterical response, especially from my sister-in-law. "I'm calling the police," Currie boomed as he made for the phone. The panic was contagious: I ran out the door and made for the mangroves a few blocks away. I knew no one would look for me, much less find me, in the mud and dense tangled growth. I spotted sheriff cars hundreds of yards in the distance, several times. Late afternoon gave way to the darkness; I was ready to make my move.

My shoes were hopelessly stuck deep in the mud, but I didn't need them. My plan was to swim the Intracoastal to Indian Rocks Beach. The waterway was about a mile across from my hideout, so without hesitation I started swimming with my slow distance style. About three-quarters of the way across, I changed course and headed to a dark area a half-mile north.

I made it to shore where I met with another muddy stand of mangroves. I felt safe and the smell of the mud, the bird leavings, and the exposed oyster beds took me back to the days of my youth when I fished and worked at the Fish House. The mud was thigh deep and it took awhile to reach a sandy beach where I could walk inland. Suddenly I realized I was in Tiki Gardens, a tourist attraction I had sneaked into in the daylight when I was a kid—on a dare to steal a peacock.

You cannot imagine what a panicked peacock sounds like—at least when you are trying to steal one. The noise in decibels seems like a train whistle, but at high C.

The park was closed, but with my night vision taking over, I wandered for hours around the two-acre attraction, carefully avoiding the peacocks. Could I catch one in the dark without the ear-splitting noise? My mania, among other things, gives me a very sharp memory and carries me quickly from one thought to another and from a bad emotion to a good one or vice versa.

Out of curiosity I looked through a window in the small building at the entrance and saw a clock on the wall: It was 3:00 a.m. The streets were empty, the shops were closed, and there wasn't a person in sight. I decided it was safe to walk south on the sidewalk.

Once past the gardens, I became aware of my appearance. Mud covered my legs up to my cutoffs, and my shirt and arms were mud-spotted as well. I entered the first condominium on the bay side of the street and stealthily reconnoitered for any sign of life. I found the swimming pool, rinsed my shirt in the shallow end, rung it out, put it on the side of the pool and proceeded to rinse off the rest of the mud. Just as I put my shorts back on, two cop cars sped around the side of the building and headed for the pool—and for me.

Without thinking I leaped out and ran at breakneck speed to a dock on the waterway. It was as if they didn't believe I would jump in. "Do you know how much trouble you're in? What kind of drugs are you on, anyway? You'll only spend a few days in jail—so come with us." All the while, they inched closer to me.

"Screw you!" I yelled as I ran to the end of the dock, dove in and started swimming until I was out of range, while swapping obscenities with the cops.

The mainland was mostly dark, so I swam toward the bridge to the south: probably a mile-and-a-half diagonally back across the waterway. I wanted to avoid the mangroves and most of the mud. It seemed to take hours.

I emerged onto the sand lit by the lights of the bridge. I had on only my cutoffs— no shoes, shirt or ID. I noticed something shining on the ground. It was a three-inch knife with most of the wooden handle eroded away by the elements. I slipped it into my pocket.

Walking the streets, I became more anxious by the moment; I had not slept for days. I ended up on a dead-end street lined by only three giant mansions on the bay side. Outside of the last one a large black or dark blue Cadillac was parked. I pulled on the back door handle and it opened. Exhausted, I climbed in and tried to get some form of sleep; it was just getting light.

Time passed slowly, but I must have fallen asleep because I was jarred awake by angry voices and the opening of the car doors. A shotgun barrel was pointed inches from my nose. With the County Sheriff deputies training several weapons on me, I had enough sense not to fight. Mercifully, I lost consciousness, just as I had done previously. I'm sure they restrained my still active body by cuffing me before they stuffed me in the back of their car.

The strip-search was the next surreal experience. Then they gave me a gray jumpsuit, a blanket, some cigarettes, soap and other necessities before leading me to a large cellblock. When I realized my cell was also home for several dozen roaches, I yelled for a guard. After thirty minutes of yelling, I realized it was to no avail.

Another inmate finally called to me and said I should light my blanket on fire—that would get rid of the roaches. Like a fool, I did so. The guards came, took my matches and blanket, and left the roaches. I did get three matches and a piece of strike board tossed to me from the guy in the next cell.

I developed a technique that allowed me to pass 80 per cent of the time in a twilight sleep. I tried to get as comfortable as possible on the hard bunk and forcibly removed all thoughts from my emotions and mind. A daily dose of Mellaril facilitated the effort.

About the end of the third week, I was taken to my Public Defender to discuss my case; the hearing was still weeks away. The attorney had just received the case and had no time to review my arrest record. I learned I was to be charged with Armed Burglary! The insignificant knife was the cause of the armed charge and trying to sleep in the back of the car was considered burglary. What should have been misdemeanor vagrancy was blown way out of proportion. This could result in a fifteen-year prison sentence. The man spent only a minute or so with me and gave me no hope.

My brothers, Ralph and Currie, spoke with me on the phone on the other side of the glassed in visiting area. For a few years afterward, I was angry because they had not provided bond or helped me obtain counsel. I was mentally ill, not a criminal. However, I came to understand how they felt toward me—sorry for me, but thinking I had to pay the price for my actions. Any ill will has long since been forgiven; on both sides, I believe.

Another four or five weeks went by and I was taken to an office next to a courtroom to meet once again with my PD. He told me he had made a deal with the State's Attorney. "Plead no contest and you'll be released immediately with only two-year's probation." At the time, I did not understand that being adjudicated guilty meant I was now, and forever would be, a convicted felon. I just wanted to be released.

In a month the jailhouse jitters disappeared with the help of my psychiatrist and a new mix of medications. I went looking for a job. Within days of filling out a State of Florida application for a position with the State Department of Education, they called me to come in for an interview.

Ralph gave me four hundred dollars so I could get a suit, and I borrowed a nephew's car—mine was repossessed while I was in jail—for my drive to Tallahassee.

I took some Xanax an hour before entering the conference room in the tall capitol building. I was so excited to see five familiar faces around the table. During some of my twelve years with the Manatee County School Board I served as District Liaison to the Department of Education. All these people remembered me from triennial meetings in Orlando, Florida and at many other sites. They even knew I had moved to Haiti.

Their questions and my answers had little to do with the job. It was not an interview, but an invitation, with a super salary, benefits and free tuition to FSU to finish my Doctorate in Urban Education Research, on office time. I was to be the second of a pair of liaisons for the sixty-seven Florida school districts—responsibilities just the reverse of my twelve-years of experience. I could start in two weeks.

On the way home, I stopped to see a friend at the Pasco County School District, where he served as superintendent. He was also the Majority Whip for the Florida House of Representatives. We worked together in the Doctoral program at USF and were great friends. He finished the program; I had left because of my refusal to do a year's teaching residency and because of my medical issues.

He was as excited to see me, as I was to see him. When I told him about the job he buzzed his secretary and told her to get the State Commissioner, on the phone. I told him they gave me a verbal offer, but he wanted to go to the top for me. For almost ten minutes he gave me high-sounding praise, not all legitimate. The job was mine I could hardly believe it.

Both a phone call and a letter arrived two days before I was to move to Tallahassee. They had to retract the offer because of my latest felony conviction. It seemed there was no use applying for a professional position anywhere else.

I moved to the dark side to find a dark job.

Twenty-seven – All Night Job

For the wretched, one night is like a thousand,
for someone faring well death is just one more night.
Sophocles

In 1990 the population of metropolitan Bradenton, Palmetto, and Sarasota was around 680,000. There were several taxi companies serving the area, but one of them was the most lucrative to work for.

The owner, was a big guy—at least 350 fifty pounds and only about five-feet, ten inches. His customers gave great tips to his drivers, and all the people of the night knew him. They trusted him to get to them quickly and take them safely home. The company's stickers were in every party place in the entire metro area.

My shift was from 6:00 p.m. to 6:00 a.m. six days a week, Monday through Saturday. Many times I was dispatched to area strip clubs, where I was expected to go in and seek out my fare, just like any other bar. Whenever the drunken partier offered me a drink, I had to decline, but I seldom turned down a free lap dance.

On one occasion I picked up one of countless crack prostitutes. She had no cash at the end of the ride, so she offered her services in exchange for the five-dollar fare; I declined.

I picked up "classier" prostitutes at their homes or apartments, drove them to their "johns," and waited just outside for the duration of their tryst.

I intervened if there seemed to be a problem and had a few altercations as a result of this arrangement. The fare and wait time was substantial, but often the twenty-five to fifty dollar tip made the trip worthwhile.

At the end of a shift we tallied our fares and turned in half to the company, keeping the remainder to refill our cab with gas. We kept all our tips. Sometimes I made over seven hundred dollars a week, but the average was about four-hundred fifty.

I knew all the crack houses in the entire area. My rule was to get a twenty-dollar bill to hold while they went inside for their smoke and then drive off with the money. I had better ways to spend it than they did. I reported the trip as a ten-dollar fare with the balance as a tip. Often, only a mile down the road, I received a call to pick up the same guy and he never knew I was the one who just took his twenty dollars. If my passengers intended to stay for sex, as well as a smoke, they paid up front and my scam didn't work.

Passengers could drink or smoke weed in the cab, but not crack—my rules. The sheriff, who knew the dispatcher, called the owner frequently asking for a driver to respond to some altercation or DUI and take a partially innocent, but completely obnoxious drunk home. The deputy asked the passenger for the fare to be paid up front—padded by ten dollars at our request. Once I had the passenger in my taxi I became the authority figure, which often resulted in verbal abuse. If the abuse became physical I knew what to do: I took a fast left turn near a grassy lawn, reached across my fare to open his door, and let the physics of the turn roll him out without my having to stop.

The first to run from me without paying his nine-dollar fare was a black man. I left my cab, and ran after him until I came to a stop among several of his friends deep in his own neighborhood. I retreated rapidly. From then on, if my profiling skills indicated I had a potential runner, I asked for my fare up front. A few would pay, but most of them I had to tell to get out of the cab.

The later the night, the thicker the roll of cash in my shirt pocket became. One taxi driver was shot in the head for his cash; this was not uncommon in the Tampa Bay area. When a passenger looked suspicious, I encouraged him to sit up front with me. I carried a tire iron and an eight-inch knife and had to use the tire iron only once. I was glad I had it when a drunken fare slowly produced a knife. I pulled the iron from between my legs, hit him hard in the chest, stopped quickly and pushed him out of the cab.

Occasionally a call came across the radio without an assigned driver—instead of the name of the next of us in the rotation. An address in a really bad section of town was accompanied with, "We should probably skip it, unless any of you guys want it." I prided myself on my volunteering to take the calls nobody else wanted and I often did out-of-town runs.

And so it went. For many months I roomed with several day drivers so we could swap shifts with the same taxi and save time. Later I bought a used 1100cc V65 Honda, making weekly payments. I rented a pleasant room in the home of a kind girl on the Westside and began to send out resumes.

Even taking my meds, I found wakening each day akin to a tragedy. The depression was intense, but I had no choice: I had to get up. Once I was behind the wheel and had a few fares under my belt, I noticed a change in my mood—spiraling upward to a hypomanic state by night's end.

People talk to taxi drivers even more than to bartenders. The intimate problems revealed required a psychologist or therapist. My circumstances, even though they were far down on the "scum scale," didn't come close to the tragic situations I heard about. I became grateful for my job, my family, and my elusive faith.

A few times I approached mania—it happens. The owner would come get me and make me go home, but he always expected me to be on the job the next evening. Other times I could hardly stay awake if I didn't have a fare. I would run off the road and be jarred awake, always without incident or any damage.

Concerned about the situation, I made an appointment to see my psychiatrist, Dr. M. He was a physician who wanted his patients to be totally involved with their medication and treatment. Still, I was surprised that he approved my request for some Dextroamphetamine to keep me awake when I needed to be, and chloral hydrate to put me to sleep at home in order to avoid a full-blown manic episode. My dad had told me that a solution of chloral hydrate in alcohol, referred to as knockout drops, was used to prepare a "Mickey Finn."

In spite of the doctor's extremely cautionary instructions, I mixed these two new drugs with my other meds; within a week I was manic. I climbed on my motorcycle and headed for Miami, hoping to get to Haiti from there and to disappear with my meager stash of cash. I had no plan, just fast-growing, fluctuating, manic ideas and a feeling of self-assurance.

The Miami police at the International Airport picked me up. I spent $160 of my hard-earned cash on a one-night stay and room service at the airport motel. Apparently my explanation for bizarre behavior at the motel didn't make sense: they sent me directly to a psych ward in Locktown.

My recollection of the horrific two-week stay is somewhat vague, but eventually the plethora of injected and oral drugs produced my keepers' idea of a moderately sane person. Jack, a taxi driver and former roommate, drove the two hundred miles to pick up me and my bike and get us back to Bradenton. I immediately went back to work driving for John.

Within a year of my felony conviction, a cousin sent me two hundred dollars and said I was to get in touch with my Public Defender again. I was required to produce my undergraduate and graduate diplomas for the judge in order for him to change my record from "adjudication guilty" to "adjudication withheld nuc pro quo." The Latin words essentially said I was no longer and never had been a convicted felon. The arrest record, like the others, remained public knowledge, but unfortunately, unless people chose to read the two felony case dispositions they would not know I was vindicated of the charges.

Twenty-eight – Dominican Republic

If you think in terms of a year, plant a seed; if in terms of ten years,
plant trees; if in terms of one hundred years, teach the people.
Confucius

When I finally received a job offer from a school for missionary dependents in the Dominican Republic, I jumped at the chance to regain some dignity. The teaching position in Santiago paid only living expenses and a small stipend. In the summer of 1992 the majority of the students were Roman Catholics, whose parents, expatriate Dominicans, had returned after having fled the country during the dictatorship of Trujillo. (He was assassinated in 1961.) I was to teach high school mathematics, computer science, and Bible theology. The kids spoke Spanish as a first language, but most also spoke English with the ease of a New Yorker and for the most part were all-American.

Santiago was a provincial city without many English-speaking tourists. Three nights a week I attended class to learn Spanish. The teacher did not speak any English, and there were only three of us students. My first try at using the language was to ask a street vendor "Quiero un perrito caliente," which literally translated means, "I want a hot dog." Although perrito is the word for dog, the Spanish word for hot dog *is* "hot dog."

My second mistake was asking a waiter where the restroom was: "Donde esta la cerveza?" He kept sending me to the bar; I was asking,

"Where's the beer?" I should have asked, "Donde son los servicios?" Spanish was an extremely difficult language for me to learn. My ability to learn and speak French Creole in a matter of months had spoiled me—no grammar, syntax or gender issues to learn. After a few months of classes I took my good-looking teacher to dinner. The conversation was limited; she kept correcting me.

The Dominican Republic is a much lovelier country than Haiti. It has mountains like Haiti, but they are covered with trees, unlike the denuded rocks that make up the mountainous terrain across all of Haiti. When I flew over from one country to the other, I could actually see the border where it changed from desolate mountains to beautiful forests. The Haitians had cut down 95% of the trees to use for charcoal to cook with.

The student population at the Santiago Christian School was around seven hundred, from grades one through twelve. I taught Algebra I and Bible to thirty eighth-graders, Computer Science (we had a well-equipped lab with twenty PCs) to ninth through twelfth-graders, and Algebra II to a mixture of tenth and twelfth-graders. Both Algebra I & II, were my forte and we all had a good time in the Computer Lab.

My two middle-school classes were large and yet the kids had manners and most listened when I threatened discipline. The high school classes were smaller and presented no discipline problems.

I got to know the staff well. Aside from the many faculty meetings, we often met in each other's homes for food and fellowship. I became special friends with Annie, a pretty, blonde fifth-grade teacher from Vancouver, B.C. We took many trips together into town to practice our Spanish and see the sights. Annie was twenty-three and I was forty, but we got along extremely well. I was attracted to her and she knew it. However, we also knew that short of an occasional electric touch, we were to practice the Virtues we taught. When we went off together for the day, she would later give an account to some of her fellow female teachers. Some of my colleagues suggested I "avoid all appearances of evil," but I think they wished they, too, could drum up some innocent female companionship.

When one of teachers in an advanced class told Annie that a teacher had declared, "Ricardo es muy simpatico," I began greeting that teacher with the traditional kisses. I was approaching hypomania and my sexual actions were uninhibited, so I asked the teacher to dinner. Annie had bet me I wouldn't. She did, however, want an accounting of the whole evening. That was the extent of my romance in the Dominican Republic.

With no television, there was nothing to do on weeknights except read, study, grade papers, and make lesson plans for the next day. So by midnight, I was in bed under the mosquito netting and a nice fan. Every night, without fail, the electricity went off until noon the next day. I had about three hours of sleep a night.

A shower in the morning consisted of a small pan with a handle dipped into extremely cold water from a five-gallon bucket. How the atmosphere could be so hot and the water so cold was a mystery.

A large green school bus made the rounds of the town picking up teachers each morning. The entire school, including faculty and staff, met at lunch under a large tree, where a small trailer sold sandwiches and snacks. Mixed groups of teachers and students sat in the shade on benches and talked about most anything.

Things could not be better. After four months I wrote a long letter to people I cared about and told them I planned to stay on in the Dominican, teaching and learning Spanish, for at least three years to prove to myself and others that I could do so without regressing mentally.

Frequently, I had pain and problems with my teeth. In Haiti I had one tooth pulled with pliers; for an anesthetic, they gave me a half-bottle of rum along with pain pills from the pharmacy. Here in the Dominican Republic I faced chronic pain until I could find a real dentist. In my effort to get some relief, I remembered a non-narcotic medication named Darvon Compound 65. The nearby pharmacy sold me sixty capsules. I took them liberally, unaware the psychiatric side effects included abnormal behavior, a confused state, and hallucinations. Nor did I know changes in mental status had been reported with the use of this drug.

By Christmas, I became disturbed and emotional for no apparent reason. My usual cocktail of prescribed medicine was being picked up and sent each month by my sister, Patty, and I took them as directed. Still, I felt paranoid and had the need to spend my two weeks' vacation at home.

I scheduled a flight out of Puerto Plata on a Mission Aviation Fellowship plane.

Once home, I had no transportation and only saw my kids once. Patty's place seemed to be closing in on me as I continued to take Darvon along with my meds. I left Bradenton before my vacation ended and took a commercial flight back into the D.R. When I arrived, I called the school director to pick me up and drive the van the forty-two miles to what I thought was home.

Nothing seemed right. I told the principal of my illness and he made an appointment for me with a psychiatrist. He went with me to translate. The doctor prescribed different medications from what I had been taking. My mania grew worse and finally the staff and psychiatrist suggested I resign. I left after completing the first semester of teaching.

Patty was the only one who would let me stay, so I lived with her and Bob for several months. I applied for Social Security Disability. Although I was very depressed, my sister's tough love approach was to declare I should get up and look for a job. She let me use her car and I found a job in Pinellas Park, north of St. Petersburg. George, the owner of a small computer firm, hired me as a programmer. I could stay in George's garage apartment, and we could find a car for me later.

Having to focus on maintaining and customizing many UNIX systems applications, both on and off line, and in and out of the state was good for my mind. I enjoyed the work, the cash payments, and trips all over Tampa Bay and out-of-state in a 1977 Chevrolet Capri. I spent the weekends with my kids in Bradenton.

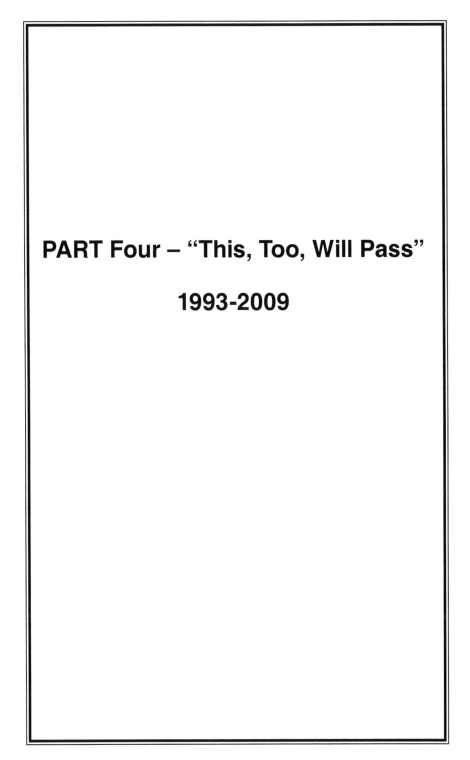

PART Four – "This, Too, Will Pass"

1993-2009

Twenty-nine – Out of the Shadows

*Mysteriously and in ways that are totally remote from
natural experience, the gray drizzle of horror induced
by depression takes on the quality of physical pain.*
William Styron

F ive months after joining George's enterprise, I received a letter from
the Social Security Administration. They had examined some ten
years of my records as a manic-depressive psychotic. During my working
career, I had a total of five years when I earned high salaries. SSA paid
me a lump sum up front and promised monthly payments each month
thereafter.

Furthermore, based on my record, I was placed in the same category as
a paraplegic; I would not be reevaluated for ten years. Had I been able to
invest all the funds I paid into Social Security, I might have accumulated
several hundred thousand dollars. Now I was simply retiring early, so I
took the deal offered me.

I gave money to Veronica for her upcoming wedding, and to Sebastian
to buy a new motorcycle. I put a down payment on a hot turbo-charged all-
wheel-drive sports car—typical hypomanic behavior. I continued working
with George for a few months.

When a speeding motorist killed my dog I had an extreme emotional
response, which lead to my admittance to the psychiatric hospital. Veronica

married David, a great guy who in later years I referred to as Saint David, but I missed the opportunity to walk my daughter to the altar. (Sebastian did the honors). I was busy being the Master of the Universe. Veronica visited me at my worst moment. She cried both for her absentee Dad, who would miss her wedding, and for me. She had never seen me in this state before.

After three weeks I was released, still a bit on the high side. Sebastian and I were sharing an apartment. He had been recently divorced from his first wife and wasn't around much.

It was February 1993; the internet was not yet in common use for meeting potential dates. I called personal ads and became involved with several women. After short flings with the first two, I went to meet a third woman whose mother had a PhD in psychology. Although I was not interested in the daughter, her mother recognized my mania and suggested I fly to Texas, and become an inpatient at a psychiatric hospital there. She seemed very familiar with this facility and insisted they could really help me. God knows why, but I did it.

I spent a month there. It was more posh than all the others, but no different when it came to administering drugs to bring me down—really deep down depressed. That was a cold winter—it even snowed in lower Texas. I managed to escape, but my journey (wherever that was to be) required some clothes. I had no cash, but I spotted a Good Will Center where I "borrowed" a sweater and jacket.

Next, I found a VFW. I walked in and ordered a drink, unabashedly pretending to be a Vietnamese war veteran. As I took the first sip, a big, smiling patient aide came in, paid for the drink, and escorted me back to the hospital.

I finally reached an excessive low, which to a mental hospital staff always meant I was cured. They released me at the Greyhound Bus Station because I could no longer afford a plane ticket. The claustrophobic surroundings and my increasing paranoia made for a horrible three-day trip back to Florida.

My car was repossessed. I had nowhere to stay but the mother and daughter's home. I slept in the top of their A-frame house, took a few meals, but had little personal contact. I gave them part of my Social Security money for the privilege.

A few months came and went before I came to my senses and called Patty. She found a small studio I could rent and was on her way to get me, although I was sixty miles north of Bradenton.

The one-room studio apartment with a bath was about twelve by thirty feet. The kitchen offered a miniature refrigerator and a two-burner stove. Cabinets, dishes and silverware were provided. In New York City this place would rent for $1800/month, but here it was only $350. A large portion of the remainder of my money went toward paying off bad checks, for which I was just short of being criminally charged. My daughter-in-law brought me a TV.

Veronica's husband, David came by almost daily and spent time talking with me. It was approaching spring of 1993. George sought me out to bring me my PC and to have me write a bar coding routine for a major client of his. David and I played solitaire; he always beat the clock. Without his daily visits, I was alone. On Sundays, Patty and Bob picked me up for church. Afterward, they gave me time at the grocery store to stock up for the next week.

This was to be my lot. There was nothing in life or in the future but endless days and nights. My depression deepened. I lit a candle night after night and tried to find solace in the Bible: I was amazed at how many saints suffered from depression and how well they could articulate their hopelessness. Still, they were never driven to the point of suicide and remained faithful to the idea "this, too, will pass." And it always did.

When alone, which was almost always, I gained great comfort in the darkness with my candle, Bible, and meditation.

In three months, I got a call from ACSI, American Communications and Supply Corporation. They needed a payroll module and the electronic ACH automatic deposit routine added to their UNIX system. I could remain focused on this and install and maintain the system via phone connection. Four weeks into this project, and another came along. The Eye Center called and asked if they could send someone for me. They needed help with several issues. This turned out to be a bi-weekly event, including some new custom work.

During this time, I realized I had gained excessive weight from the effects of Lithium on my thyroid, not eating properly, and living a sedentary lifestyle. I knew I needed to make some changes. In less than a year I lost over a hundred pounds through a low calorie diet, meditation, and daily exercise at the gym with David. Without David's encouragement and friendship I would not have made it.

Where had the motivation come from? I was still swinging between depression and hypomania. Mental, spiritual, and physical exercise and diet became habitual. I was now wearing a medium-size shirt and thirty-two waist jeans. Ripples of muscle showed through the thin skin on my arms and my chest. My hair grew well below my shoulders; even my son, Sebastian, made positive mention of my physical change.

I saved and bought a car, a vintage '73 Cougar for fifteen hundred dollars. It was in great shape and had a Big Block Cleveland V8 that I could work on— no extra mess like the engines in the new cars. Purpose, focus, and faith became constant, despite the extreme highs and lows. The steady income was medicine for my anxiety.

In early 1995, Veronica introduced me to one of her girlfriends, Marie. David and I had just come from the gym and I was dressed in black sweatpants and a black tank top. With my dark beard—courtesy of Just for Men—and flowing dark brown hair, it was hard to picture me as Veronica's dad. After all, there were only sixteen years between our ages.

Marie was thirteen years younger than I was. She was beautiful, gentle, and sweet. She had glorious natural brown hair, with superb brown eyes that matched her adorably sweet smile. I was in love immediately—even before she stood up and revealed an equally lovely figure.

Marie and her sister met Veronica several weeks prior when a massage therapist had recommended her as a good nail tech. Both Marie and Barb had been impressed when Veronica spoke so often and so well of her father and suggested Marie should meet her dad. She was already trying to set me up. My baby girl.

Veronica brought us together for our first meeting, and then suggested we three take a walk. It was cold outside but we bundled up. The conversation was mostly girl-talk: I listened patiently.

The next week Veronica called and said Marie was coming over for a pedicure. I decided to stop by and ask her out for lunch. We took a remote booth at the Olive Garden and spent at least two hours talking. I had learned long ago to let my date speak and if things got slow, to ask questions.

I stopped dating altogether except for Marie. I began the ritual of picking her up at her house, going out for the evening, and returning for intimate fellowship into the night. She had a bad first marriage and was somewhat vulnerable. I courted her properly—flowers, gifts for her, and dog treats for her little dog.

Two months into our relationship, she surprised me with a proposal to spend a week together in St. Augustine. We had a blast during our trip, and on the way home Jeannie surprised me again; she asked me to move in with her and get out of that dumpy little place I was living in. A year or so prior nobody could have convinced me that my future would change so drastically.

Marie had a BS in Business from Stephens College, a small elite women's college in Missouri. Since graduation, she had been working as a billing clerk for a group of periodontists. It was a thankless and minimum paying job, but she was a people-person so she enjoyed it. A client of mine was interested when I told them of my new girlfriend. Marie and I prepared her résumé and noted she also had computer skills. Furthermore, if she needed any help, I would not charge for the privilege. They hired her as Office Manager at a higher wage, more in keeping with her training. She was to manage some twenty-five women, clerks and techs—no small task.

I came to the office in early May with a beautiful 1-Carat, F-clarity, VVS1 bridal set and proposed marriage and a date for the event. I had to borrow two of the three thousand dollars from Patty and Bob. In her first marriage she had to buy her own ring; I knew giving her this ring would impress and please her. She accepted.

We were married on 31 May 1995, my forty-fourth birthday.

As a self-respecting new husband, I had to get off disability. Marie knew all about my history and said it was not necessary, but I felt differently.

My first interview with *INC Magazine's* number three fastest growing firm in the U.S. resulted in my being hired on the spot. It was an electronic engineering firm in Sarasota. I became their IT Director for over thirty engineers, a manufacturing staff of at least 375, plus the accounting department. Apparently they did not do background searches on potential staff members.

With each of us earning a good salary and neither of us inclined to cook dinner; we dined out almost every night. We both enjoyed our beer and good food; it was like a date every night. Just as on our first date, we talked for hours, never running out of conversation. We were whole-heartedly in love. As Marie liked to remark frequently, we were soul mates.

Thirty – One Long Date

So long as we love, we serve; so long as we are loved by others,
I should say that we are almost indispensable;
and no man is useless while he has a friend.
Robert Louis Stevenson

Everyone in my family, and all who met Marie wherever she went, treasured her friendship immediately. She had a beautiful smile and personality and her pleasant, chatty conversation style exhibited friendly affection to everyone she encountered.

To me she was the very *Gift of God* to my body, soul and spirit. The details of our marriage and life together for the first six years are too poignant for me to put in writing. Suffice it to say that it was the most splendid and joyful period of my entire life—like one long date. This, of course was my perception. I believe Marie's non-confrontational personality made it a joy for her also, but only for the first few years. The vicissitudes of my illness were never in complete remission and during those years some rather drastic things occurred.

One can be told about a loved one's manic depression, but never really understand until a high or low episode occurs within the confines of the relationship. Unfortunately, all my negative attributes—excessive pride, arrogance, inflated self-esteem, and egotism—had weathered the storms of the humiliating indignity and shame I'd experienced over the prior twenty years.

Within the first year, for example, we were driving home from my daughter's. I began a dogmatic and angry harangue about some unimportant issue that had nothing to do with us. Marie was silent. My remarks were not directed toward her; I was sure she agreed with me on the subject. When I happened to glance over at her, she had tears rolling down her face. She had a very tender spirit. I apologized but the damage was done. I purposed never to raise my angry voice again. By the time we got home, she seemed herself and I had forgotten what I had gone on about. I was so ashamed, and I told her so. Lovingly, she assured me she forgave me.

As with Helen and Bonnie before her, I supposed my marriage to Marie would be for life. Our separation when I had worked in Costa Rica for a time seemed to make our hearts grow fonder.

Good jobs were hard to get in Florida. Out-of-state employers apparently were not concerned with doing a background search. I took a regional IT Director's job in Baltimore, after Marie agreed to come with me. I felt I had no choice.

We found a place in Maryland, sold the house in Bradenton, and shipped all our furniture up. Then Marie decided to stay behind. Her family had convinced her to stay in Florida. She began studying for her RN, but she could have done so in Maryland at Johns Hopkins University and interned at the hospital there.

My work took me to Washington in 2001. We took turns flying back and forth every third weekend until 9/11; I felt the ground shake when the aircraft hit the Pentagon. It was several months afterward before Marie or I could get a flight. My archenemies—loneliness and depression—attacked with unusual intensity. In anger I quit the IT job; my performance was less than adequate, I probably would have been asked to resign soon anyway.

I found a teaching job on the internet that very afternoon. I was contacted by the principal of a parochial high school located between Andrews AFB and D.C., interviewed the next morning, and was hired immediately as a teacher of computer science. I taught six periods a day.

Most of my students were quite disciplined; they were sons and daughters of military personnel. Other parents worked in various government positions. This was probably the only job I could hold in my period of dark melancholy. I worked the entire school year with the exception of the first few weeks; I had been hired quickly because they had no teacher in place at the beginning of the year. My salary dropped by $20,000 from that of the IT position in D.C.

I looked forward to Marie's visits or when I joined her in Florida. In retrospect, I believe she was glad when they were over; in my downhearted state, I was not good company at all. One time she even suggested that instead of meeting her, I should take the train to New York and spend the weekend with her older sister at her Ten Park Avenue apartment. On Friday, two miles from the school, I boarded the train and came out at Penn Station, two blocks from Barb's apartment; it beat going through the airports to make the round trip to Florida.

Barbara had been Miss Indiana and first runner-up to Miss America in 1977. She married a famous novelist and movie screenplay writer. She was divorced and living on a huge settlement. We spent the weekend running around on the subway, shopping, movie going, dining and visiting Ground Zero. The activity temporarily relieved my disheartened mood. I disembarked the train early Monday morning in time for school.

When I had left Baltimore, I put all our furniture in storage and found a roommate near Annapolis—a forty-five minute drive to school. Marie and I talked on the phone most every night. My poor mood was not nearly as apparent over the phone. I also had Buddy, the cocker spaniel Marie had given me as a puppy the Christmas of 1995. He was actually Buddy III, the first stayed with Bonnie and a car killed the second. I came to love this Buddy as much as my family. I felt his unconditional love in return. He would never leave my side, leash or not.

I flew to Florida for Christmas. Marie and I spent two weeks together in a nice romantic apartment on the bay in St. Petersburg. This should have been perfect for us to renew our love and for me to make every effort to reconcile, but my black-mood symptoms made it impossible. I had lost interest or found no pleasure in activities that I once enjoyed, including sex. This surely made Marie feel unloved. My fatigue, decreased energy, feelings of hopelessness, pessimism, guilt, worthlessness, helplessness, restlessness, and irritability undoubtedly contributed to a less than desirable time together.

No one can enjoy being stuck with such a gloomy individual, but Marie never stopped smiling. The two weeks went very slowly for me and probably much slower for her. I flew back to Maryland the second day of 2002 with the sensation I was watching myself act, while having no control over the situation.

In the spring, we had a week together in Bradenton. I recall battling the same feelings as the last extended visit together. These two visits were made tolerable by spending time with my kids and their families and with Marie's sisters, mother and grandmother.

It was decided Marie would get an apartment for us in Bradenton. So early in June she joined me in Annapolis to help pack our belongings in a large U-Haul truck. We tied my car behind us for the trip back to Bradenton. I was hopeful for the future—a new beginning.

With the help of her sister Barb, the Feng shui designer, Marie had created a psychedelic lime and pink apartment, studded with flowered trim. She waited for me to be amazed and pleased with our new surroundings. I felt it was done just for me. Marie was excited and proud—a new place for a new start.

My depression was serious, but controllable. I was physically capable of the hard work required to move in, but my extreme fatigue, one of the symptoms of depression, made me appear lazy to her family members. They were helping us move what seemed to be a mountain of contents up winding stairs to the second-story apartment. This, I'm sure, did not help future relations; it was viewed as a character flaw—at least by her grandmother.

After we settled in, I applied to Clearwater Central Catholic High School to teach algebra and geometry. I had taught a full year there some twenty years before. The Mother Superior—with her white Sisters of Notre Dame habit covering all but her face—had been a close friend and a fellow teacher. I was surprised to find the habits replaced with casual attire. She remembered me and hired me for the 2003-4 school year, apparently ignoring my background check.

I spent four months, cycling rapidly back and forth between good days and bad ones. Sometimes I was "super teacher," other times hardly able to think. Years before, when I lectured at Nova University in Measurement and Statistics, I had one class of eighty-five and another of forty. Some days I could see the lights of understanding in my student's eyes, sometimes, complete anxiety and dullness. My psychiatrist suggested I tape my lectures. This was very revealing to me. On the good days I was completely and continuously understandable. On the bad days, I was surprised to realize I had only *thought* of every other phrase but failed to *speak* it. My mind was going much faster than my ability to articulate. While delivering the lecture, I was sure I had been speaking coherently, but I was not. This symptom of hypomania reappeared while teaching these young students of mathematics.

I commuted forty-five miles each way and by the time I got home, I was usually exhausted. Having spent eleven or twelve hours teaching and traveling, I had no desire to grade tests and homework or to contact parents by email or phone.

The department head evaluated one of my geometry classes and gave me high praise. However, when she observed one of my algebra classes I was manic. I was thinking up workable problems in my head as I went along, drilling the class, and asking for associated properties all at the same time. Individual students answered without being called on. As I sped up the process I proved my exceptional mathematical skills, but earned a low evaluation due to the lack of order and discipline in the thirty-student classroom.

By the time I had fallen sufficiently behind in communicating with parents, they called me in and asked me to resign, citing I was not entirely stable. I understood.

This began a long job search within a hundred-mile radius. The few times I was invited to interview I was given the job only to have the offer retracted due to my background search.

Marie had finished her RN internship and worked as a Hospice nurse. When she came home each day, I would be sitting at my PC sending resumes and scouring job sites for possibilities, but with nothing to show for it. I knew this was a great disappointment to her. I increased my radius to all of Florida and the Southeast. Nothing came up over the months of effort. I always kept good books and had a chart of our two incomes. I had earned eighty-five per cent of all our income to date, including this lengthy dry spell. I thought that should count for something; apparently in Marie's mind it did not.

The first action on her part was to ask me to leave. I pleaded to stay and was successful by telling her I would go back to driving a taxi, which was a horrible sacrifice on my part. The darkness of six twelve-hour night shifts was the furthest desire in my current state of depression. I was back in a cab that very evening; they always needed cab drivers.

Other than on my day off, I saw Marie at 6:30 a.m. for an hour or so. I was always in a better mood when coming off a shift. It had something to do with my sleep cycle, I'm sure. I would wake her and show her the cash. We had fun counting it and breaking records as I related to her the stories of the night.

This went on for three months as I continued to send out resumes. I was asked to interview for a job in nearby Okeechobee, teaching at-risk girls from Dade county and surrounding areas.

It was a large ranch miles from any civilization; these girls, from grade eight to grade twelve were criminal offenders. I was to teach mathematics and take care of the computer network throughout the camp. I would live on the ranch and spend the weekends with Marie in Bradenton. I was straightforward with the principal concerning my arrest record. She assured me it would not be a problem; she had a record too.

Once I was convinced I had the job in spite of my record, I quit the taxi job and waited for the paperwork to go through. This took several weeks and I waited at home. I jumped through many hoops with waivers and scrutiny from the State, only to be passed over by one bureaucrat due to my record. I could sense Marie's frustration. Not that I couldn't get a job, but that I was becoming hypomanic and angry. She could not take it any longer. I left August of '04, just as I had done at the end of my prior two marriages.

Thirty-one – Before the Mast

He that will learn to pray, let him go to sea.
George Herbert

I felt free and hypomanic once I left Marie. I was alone, except for my dog Buddy, and sensed all manner of opportunity opening up to me. We were walking among the hundreds of sailboats near the municipal pier in St. Petersburg. Many were for sale or charter. A plan was forming in my mind.

At that moment, the Dean of Everglades University called me on my cell phone to inquire if I would teach a six-week undergraduate math class starting in about a week. I told her I would do it. When I hung up, I realized I had plenty of time to formulate my plan.

By the time I completed the six weeks in December of 2004, I had found an entry on the internet under "used sailboats." The one I chose was the same model I had lived on at the Yacht Club for a while between my marriages to Helen and Bonnie.

This sailboat was located just south of Baltimore in an Annapolis boat yard. The one that had served as my home was a 1973 Catalina 27 that was still sailing well into the 2000s. The advertised boat was a 1984 model Catalina 27, with inboard motor, all sails, and a list of other needed equipment included. The current owner's father, a US Naval officer who retired 1984, used the boat as a cruising yacht in the summer months only.

It was dry-docked all winter. He gave it to his son in 2002, who, along with his Aussie friend Art, added sails, removed all unnecessary gear from the interior and started racing it. Now that the son wanted to sell it, he agreed to put all the cruising items back on the boat.

I told the owner I would be up in a week to take possession of the boat. He had answered my questions satisfactorily. It was December 17, 2004; even Buddy was excited. Spending most of my life in the tropics, I was not thinking how cold and stormy it can get in the more northern latitudes, nor did I realize that by the end of December most marinas closed all the way south to Florida. In my mental state these were but mere details.

The actual temperature when I arrived was 19°F and in the upper Chesapeake Bay the water was near freezing. I was told the winds had been a steady 20-25 knots and a Nor'easter was on its way—details I didn't bother about.

When I first checked out my boat, there was a foot of snow covering the deck. We took a short shakedown cruise as Art pointed out various idiosyncrasies so I could avoid learning the hard way. Back at the dock I signed seventy hundred-dollar Traveler's checks and Art gave me a bill of sale. After purchasing twelve hundred dollars worth of necessary equipment and provisions, Buddy and I left at dawn the next morning, when the winds were a bit lighter—maybe 12-15 knots.

Hypomanics articulate convincingly, and achieve beyond what they could do in an ordinary state. In discussing my fears, at least three of my psychiatrists said I preferred death to boredom. I sensed this trip of fifteen hundred miles would not be boring.

December 19, 2004 the temperature dropped to 17°F. The water temperature in the Bay was still 35°. The northerly wind had increased to 20-25 knots in the unprotected waters in the river.

Some short tacks out the mouth of the Severn River—past the Naval Academy—and a beam reach of six miles, put me in the Chesapeake. A turn south and I was wing-and-wing, using the spinnaker pole with a hanked on Kevlar 170 percent racing Genoa, jenny or foresail to hold it portside. We were quickly up to six knots—boat-speed. Having spent a great deal of time racing, I now tried to trim the sails for another quarter-knot. The boom vang held both the boom and mainsail parallel to the deck on starboard and kept it from jibbing—the sudden and dangerous crossing over to port, possibly causing damage or knocking someone overboard.

The boat was stable with a five-foot keel, but when running before the wind it is easy to underestimate the wind speed. I held a SSE course for several hours as the western shore disappeared. I wore almost everything I brought with me: Long underwear, thin canvas pants, two pair of jeans, three flannel shirts and an entire set of foul-weather gear. My dog and first mate, Buddy, wore a thick wool sweater and a doggie lifejacket hooked on the back with a long lifeline. He stayed low in the cockpit by my feet, or below in the cabin out of the weather. We were on our way.

I knew that Kevlar was stronger than Dacron, but my jenny sail was huge and designed for light air. The wind and seas were building. Running downwind can lull a sailor into a false sense of security. The winds were building, the seas behind us were up to eight feet, and before I could decide if it was time to take down the jenny, it burst with a loud crack. I quickly turned into the wind, removed the tiller-pilot and let the main run.

The noise of the luffing sail, the waves assaulting the boat, and a raw headwind wind formed a deafening cacophony. I had a safety harness on board to keep me from being separated from the boat should I fall overboard. This contraption is belted tightly about the shoulders and chest with a heavy-duty bungee attached at the sternum, which shrinks to three feet and can extend as much as ten feet. The bungee has a clip on the end, so as one moves forward he can easily unclip, move, hold, and clip repeatedly until he reaches his destination, makes a final clip, and works with both hands.

I had never used a safety harness before and it never entered my mind to put it on. I crawled forward like a monkey on a trampoline with my head down to avoid the loose, thrashing boom and swung my body from stay to shroud to halyard until I could kneel near the bow and hold the bow pulpit with one hand.

The sheets and halyard were loosened sufficiently, so I began pulling down and loosening the hanks on the sail of the forestay—one foot at a time. With the luffing sail assaulting me from both sides, I felt I was in a snowstorm. Once I had the sail down, I removed the halyard and tack of the sail, switched the tack of the halyard to a snap-shackle, and tied the sheets. Now that the sail was completely detached from the boat, my intent was to stuff it down the forward hatch. At that moment, the boat pitched and I slid across the slippery sail and fell overboard.

If I had been entertaining any thoughts of suicide, now was the time to let nature take its course. The water seemed to burn as it quickly soaked through my clothes. I would be dead in twenty minutes or so unless I drowned first. My dog! What would happen to Buddy?

Down in the trough of the wave I could see only the mast. When at the crest I watched the boat repeatedly heave back and forth, first only a few yards away, then closer. Adrenaline must have kicked in. In my boots and layers of heavy clothing, I began swimming toward the boat. The deck looked as though a "Chinese fire drill" had taken place. A couple of lines were hanging from the deck in a semicircle, most likely a jenny sheet or halyard that I had tied off loosely but securely. After riding over maybe five sets of waves, I was able to grab a sheet amidships.

The bow has the only place on the boat that the lifelines ran down to the deck. I pulled myself forward and grabbed the lower part of the heavy aluminum pulpit. The boat was climbing to the top of the waves and plunging what seemed to be ten feet. My only hope was to pull myself aboard just after the crest passed. After several tries and I found myself on the foredeck, lying on my back on the wonderful, hard deck. The sail had blown overboard. I thanked God for the experience and the rescue, and within five minutes, I was able to start the cleanup and straightening process before getting underway.

We had lost an hour due to the incident with the jenny. The main alone was more than enough sail to give maximum speed. I set the mainsail and automatic pilot and went below where the stove had heated the cabin to a warm forty-five degrees. I took all my clothes off, jumped into the sleeping bag, got Buddy under the cover with me and hugged him close.

The safety harness was hanging from a hook on the bulkhead in front of me. My mind was racing as I contemplated how deadly the consequences of my overboard experience could have played out. As my body slowly warmed, I realized I should look for some shelter and a way to dry my clothes. I pulled the laptop on the dinette close to me, remaining in my warm bunk. I scanned the chart from my current position. Before I went overboard we had made only twenty-six nautical miles—all maritime distances are stated as nautical miles. (One nautical mile=1.15077945 miles, a unit of length corresponding approximately to one minute of arc of latitude along any meridian). There was a marina about eight miles on a WSW course. I decided to wear the harness all the time, even while sleeping, just to get used to it.

To block the wind I put on the only pair of pants remaining in the locker, added the jacket of my four-hundred dollar suit, a t-shirt, the harness, and the slowly drying foul weather gear.

I went up on deck, and reset the tiller pilot to 101°, set the main for a broad reach toward the western shore to Breezy Point Marina and went below to my sack. I watched our six-to-seven knot progress on the GPS so I could know when to prepare for docking. The beam run made it difficult to stay in the starboard bunk, the boat was heeling twenty-five to thirty-five degrees and the waves were attacking the beam. The size of Buddy's brown eyes registered his fear of this new state of gravity. I strapped us in, held him close and in a few minutes, he was asleep.

An hour passed. I climbed up to the cockpit, started the diesel, waited for it to warm up, and then let it idle in forward. Wearing my safety harness, I carefully clung to the mast and hooked the harness to the very substantial spinnaker-pole ring. I had both hands free to take down the mainsail.

We had only made thirty-five miles the first day. With sails secured, we motored into the small breakwater and relished the peace and comfort it afforded from the wind and sea. Scores of dry-docked boats in storage surrounded the sparsely filled marina for winter. I tied up in a slip near the entrance and went for a walk with Buddy. It became obvious the marina was devoid of any life except for me and my dog. It was only four o'clock in the afternoon.

I had dropped my cell in the water while docking after the shakedown cruise with Art, but purchased another just before we left. This one I kept below deck so I would not lose it in what I thought was the unlikely chance I would fall overboard. I used the Streets version of another GPS to see how far I was from anyone I knew when I had worked in D.C. I was southeast of D.C. but only thirty-one miles from Bowie, MD. After climbing to the second floor of the marina building to get a signal, I called some friends. They were fine folks who, among other outings, spent a week with Marie and me in a cabin in North Carolina; I worked with Harry on IT problems. They immediately drove down in two cars; one to leave for me to use since I was not sure where I was going. Karen took back my wet clothes to wash and dry.

It was an extremely cold night on the boat. When I awoke, Buddy's nose was expelling dragon-like frost right in my ear. When I moved off the bunk, I heard a shrieking crack. I went above deck. The marina waters were covered with ice. I had noticed from the chart the marina was at the mouth of a freshwater creek.

After a cup of coffee for me and breakfast for Buddy, we drove off in the car, heater blasting, to find more clothes and better heat sources for the boat. I bought an additional set of clothes, including long underwear, thick wool socks, new boots, and two propane space heaters with a case of twenty-four propane canisters. I knew propane formed heat, water, and carbon dioxide when it burned and should not be used in small, unventilated spaces. I thought we would be okay as long as I kept Buddy up off the cabin floor where the CO2 settles, and opened all hatches a few inches along with the deck vents.

While I was running around making my purchases, I got a call from the dean at Everglades. She wanted me to teach a class of MBA students in statistical/quantitative methods in business. It would start in two weeks. I told her what I was about at the moment, but said I would call her back in a day or two.

Harry returned to my boat with clean, dry backup clothes. Buddy and I took off for the next stop about forty-five miles downwind. A bit late in the day we were underway off the western coast of the Chesapeake, when we encountered the familiar waves and wind. We made good time to the mouth of the Potomac River, gave a wide birth to the shallows on the north side, and continued up-river on the lee side to find an anchorage out of the wind and waves. It was dark— no moon or stars—when I dropped the hook. It had been an uneventful sail but exciting nonetheless.

According to my inside/outside thermometer it was 25º degrees outside and 28º in the cabin. We battened the hatches, started the space heaters and over the next three hours watched the inside temperature rise to 43º and no further.

I heated some canned chili and Buddy enjoyed a small bit of soft dog food, which he preferred to the dry. We dined, I checked the charts, turned out the lights and we hit the bunk together.

I lay there thinking. We needed to dock somewhere to get a new Genoa made—one to fit the cockpit-controlled roller-furling gear, which the last owner never used when he raced. If I'd had the cruising gear the first day, I would not have fallen overboard.

It was seventy-three miles SSE to Norfolk; surely, they would have a marina still open. I counted at least thirty-seven marinas in the general area of my chart. If we got underway by four in the morning, and the winds stayed strong at about thirty knots, we could make it before dark.

We waited for coffee and breakfast until we had covered the twelve miles at a beam-reach to put us back into the Bay. We turned to a more southerly course running down wind. With the pilot set we could get some grub, lie down to rest, turn the heat back up, and watch the GPS navigate us. We passed the markers at the speed of five-to-nine knots. The waves pushed and pulled back at our stern repeatedly.

We were halfway beaten to death by four-thirty that afternoon when we cruised by the shipyard southward and up into the Elizabeth River about eight miles. I stopped at the first boatyard and marina where I saw activity. There was evidence of a recent large snowstorm with tall drifts of snow everywhere. I filled my diesel tank and asked for a slip to rent. They gave me a nice sheltered slip after learning of my plans to return to Florida for seven or eight weeks.

During the winter, the office maintained a small contingent of workers and the owner of the marina. He gave me the phone number of Dave, a fifth generation sail maker. When he came to measure I told him I wanted a heavy 150 per cent Genoa to fit the existing roller-furling gear. He made his necessary measurements, made suggestions, and told me it would take him six weeks; he had other projects ongoing. The charge would be $1,300. I also called a diesel mechanic and made a date for eight weeks later. I called EU to let the dean know I would be there to teach the class. My funds were running low.

Buddy and I rented a car and headed for Florida on New Year's Eve. It was thoughtless of me to be away from my kids and grandkids at Christmas and they let me know it.

Thirty-two – Storm at Sea

Men go abroad to wonder at the heights of mountains,
at the huge waves of the sea, at the long courses of the rivers,
at the vast compass of the ocean, at the circular motions of the stars,
and they pass by themselves without wondering.
Saint Augustine

I was operating under near-manic hypomania, so it was easy to remember all my mathematics and statistics and create outlines for my lectures. However the actual teaching process stalled because of my emotional state.

This was the most difficult course in the curriculum. To add to that, my mind raced, and I spoke too quickly neglecting to articulate everything I intended to say. This made for a poor classroom experience for both my students and me. After two weeks, I decided to have the class of bright MBA students read a chapter before each meeting. They were to attempt the problems, and I would entertain questions during the long class periods. Having to think on my feet slowed me down a bit and we began to have some success. My not preparing for class essentially made for better instruction.

The six-week course went quickly and successfully. I turned in all my paperwork to the dean and let her know it would be a while before I could teach another class.

Buddy and I took my car and returned to Norfolk, and the *Off Duty*. Renaming a boat *is* considered bad luck, so I kept the original. Dave fitted the new sail—it was perfect. Now I could furl the sail up to zero square feet from the cockpit or let out full sail just as easily.

With the diesel checked over and maintenances performed, we were ready to continue our journey. For two-hundred dollars I bought an old, but sturdy, wooden dinghy I found when I walked Buddy through the boat yard. As I was planning to leave, a sailboat captain I met advised against my plans to take to the Atlantic. Winds could increase to fifty knots and waves to thirty-five feet. I would be on a beam reach for at least seventy-five miles before I could turn safely to the south and clear the Cape by a thin margin. He told me that rounding Cape Hatteras in winter would be crazy.

Sailing that far on a beam reach would beat us to death – but I *was* crazy. He described what he would do under the circumstances. He would take the Elizabeth River southeastward to either the Intracoastal Waterway or southwestward to the twenty-two-mile-long Great Dismal Swamp Canal to open waters in North Carolina. A second choice offered wide-open bays and rivers to sail, but I would have to motor the canal. At the time, I was not completely manic so I choose the canal.

We left the Waterside Marina early on Monday, February 21, 2005 and headed for the Canal. The canal's northern lock was an hour away. When we arrived, we blew our horn and waited.

Once we were in the lock, the lonely operator welcomed us. It had been eight days since the last boat had gone through. As we rose some twenty feet, we enjoyed the man's history lesson on the canal. He told me that in May 1763, George Washington made his first visit to the Great Dismal Swamp and suggested draining it and digging a north-south canal through it to connect the waters of the Chesapeake Bay in Virginia and Albemarle Sound in North Carolina. President George Washington agreed with Virginia Governor Patrick Henry: Canals were the easiest answer for an efficient means of internal transportation. The President urged their creation and improvement to avoid the dangers of Cape Hatteras. The lock keeper went on and on, but that is about all I remember.

He advised me to watch for tree limbs that might hit my mast and to stay in the center as much as possible. It was a weird trip and aptly named Dismal; the canal is very narrow and straight as a stick.

Two miles from the end of the canal we crossed the Virginia-North Carolina State Line. Once we were in the two large bodies of water, first Albemarle Sound and further, on the Pamlico Sound, sailing was great with many overnight anchorages available. Even the Intracoastal Waterway—separated from the Atlantic—was easily sailed for many miles with places to dock and get a good dinner and more beer. All these stops along the way made Buddy happy.

More than 250 nautical miles and six days from the exit lock on the Canal, we arrived at Southport, North Carolina. We docked the boat in an empty slip beside the little motel where we stayed when we drove back to Norfolk. We enjoyed two days rest and regular meals. I watched myself in the mirror weaving back and forth as my body tried to adjust to land once again.

Across the river to the west was Cape Fear. It was my intention to make passage through the Cape inlet to the Atlantic. I wanted to reach St. Augustine, Florida in one leg of about four-hundred miles. The reported winds were twenty-five to thirty-five knots and waves were ten to twelve feet. Running down wind would be fast and safe, I believed.

Once we cleared the Cape and Oak Island Western Bar, I set a heading of 202.6° SSW and with a NNE wind; I knew it would be one wild ride running before the wind.

I unfurled the jenny and the main, but it was too much sail. It took only forty-five seconds to douse the jenny with my roller-furling gear and new sail. So I used only the mainsail with the boom vang to hold it down. I went below and climbed in the bunk with Buddy; the temperature outside was forty-eight degrees. Inside, with one heater, it got up to a comfortable sixty-five degrees.

When I again watched the GPS navigate, we were traveling from four knots to twelve knots. We rode the waves up gracefully, rising slowly then plunging fast as they repeatedly pushed and drew back at our stern. The GPS was registering over-the-ground speed, not across the water. I guessed an average might get close to our overall speed. The Gulf Stream at this time a year could be against us by four or five knots. We were making close to six knots forward progress. Dead reckoning had us anchoring in St. Augustine in fifty to sixty hours if the wind held—or so I estimated.

About twenty hours out at 3:00 a.m., a thunderstorm started pounding us. I open the hatch; it was black as tar outside until a flash of lighting revealed a heart-stopping site. I was not paying attention to the GPS, but the waves were now at least twenty feet and the wind whistled through the rigging at what seemed to be gale force. The racing main did not have reef points to reduce the main sail, which were more than called for in this situation.

I could do nothing but go below, close the hatch and pray that the boat would hold together – we were at least a hundred miles off the Georgia coast by now. Buddy reflected my fear, his eyes seemed bigger than silver dollars. I held him in the bunk and we waited

We were now making less than three knots as we rode up these huge waves and fifteen knots as we came down. The boat could easily broach and roll, and come up with no mast. The fear was exhilarating as I put our life jackets on and tied Buddy to me. I tried the radio, but could find no one within the one-hundred-fifty-mile range and normal channels. I reassured myself by thinking of the ton of ballast below in the keel, and the heavy stays and shrouds. The tiller-autopilot I bought was for a much larger boat, but still worked far beyond its specifications.

Then I heard loud luffing. We either had begun to broach or were now somehow facing into the wind. I did not have time to check the compass. I opened the three slats of the hatch and looked to see what was going on. The boom had broken where the boom vang was attached. Without forward motion, we were at the mercy of the sea. We pitched, dove and came straight back up at a sixty degrees. The lightening continued to allow me a look at the seas around us. This must be something like seeing God, I thought.

I jumped into the cockpit, disconnected the autopilot and attached my harness to the portside lifeline. I made it forward to the mast, sometime airborne. I took down the mainsail and disconnected it from the boom and mast. I threw the sail below and then disconnected the two parts of the boom and tied them to several stations. I reset the pilot for due south and started the diesel full bore.

As I re-entered the cabin I slipped on some diesel fuel that had seeped up from the bilge and hit my head on the galley counter. I was out. When I came to, I tried to pack the large mainsail away. I went to the computer and began a search for where I might head. The top of Florida, the St. Mary's River, was almost due west. I got the exact course, went up to reconnect the autopilot set it 280.19 degrees with 103 nautical miles to travel.

As we turned abaft of the wind and waves came across the starboard side, we rolled from side to side, so I unfurled a small bit of the jenny. This wasn't good for the sail, but by doing so it steadied us somewhat in the huge waves.

I went below with Buddy and hit the bunk. I was very drowsy, not normal for me. I believe I had a concussion. That was my last thought before I drifted off.

Thirty-three – Heading Home

Poetry is a sort of homecoming.
Paul Celan

By the Grace of God I awoke and discovered I had been asleep for over twelve hours. I looked outside and saw that I was right between two large ocean-going channel markers. I rechecked my course; we had traveled eighty-seven miles and I now needed to change course slightly to 275.25° to get between the markers and straight to the mouth of the river. As dull as I was, I questioned the fact of the large markers. The first one I found was in sixty-five feet of water with a channel much deeper in between. This was for freighters and tankers, what were they doing leading toward a small river like the St. Mary? I dozed off with that on my mind.

Two hours later, I was awakened by a thunderous noise from above the boat. I slid the top of the hatch back, looked above and saw a Navy helicopter with a man descending in a harness. When he saw me, he began yelling, "Hard to Port. Hard to Port."

I tried to explain my head injury and he yelled louder, "I don't give a rat's ass, HARD TO PORT!"

I jumped out into the cockpit and looked forward. A gigantic nuclear sub, eight stories high and pushing a fifteen-foot bow wake was no less than a hundred yards away and on a collision course with us. Without hesitation, I disconnected the tiller-pilot and manually made a quick turn to port. We avoided the collision by twenty feet or so. That explained the large markers: the river to the north led to Kings Bay Naval Submarine Base. This base is home to the U.S. Atlantic Fleet's Navy of Ballistic Missile nuclear submarines armed with Trident missile weapons—it had no time to wait on me.

Had the Navy man not descended to physically remove me or get my attention when he did, my boat, Buddy and I would be at the bottom of the channel and the sub would be on its way without a scratch.

We continued to head south down the Waterway and within a half-mile a welcomed sign pointing west said, "Marina." I turned into the narrow inlet. The marina was small with no evidence of life. It was about 7:00 a.m. Saturday, so I tied up at the main dock, took Buddy for a necessary walk and went below to sleep.

I awakened to a friendly knock on my deck and a "Hello, anyone aboard?"

An elderly gentleman greeted me. After talking a bit, it became apparent he was not with the marina staff, but was a live-aboard guest. When he alluded to the fact that it was Monday, I was surprised and hopeful that the forty-eight-hour sleep had helped my head injury; I did feel better. Buddy needed food and a walk, so I called him up from below, detached his safety line, and we toured the marina.

The broken boom was my main concern. Would I have to order a new one from California? The catalog in the main office told the story. It would require a seven-week delivery time and $1150 plus shipping. When I told the dock master my problem he said there were two Swedes just up the road who did extensive aluminum welding—thank God.

In a few days they had the boom securely repaired for a hundred dollars. I reinstalled it, jerry-rigged the boom vang, and we were off early the next morning, leaving the way we arrived, diligently watching for any large shipping.

We motored east until we were in fifty feet of water and six miles off shore. The winds were only 15-25 knots, the waves a maximum seven feet, and the temperature fifty-five degrees. I hoisted sail and made cautious course of 168.44° to stay offshore and give wide berth to the St. Johns River where I knew aircraft carriers, among other large vessels, were known to make seaward frequently. It was fifty-three miles to a course change toward the offshore marker to the St. Augustine Inlet.

By dusk, without incident, we were anchoring near the Lions Bridge a hundred yards from a marina, where we could tie up our dinghy for two dollars a day. The next morning Buddy and I enjoyed sightseeing until he got tired. We stopped and bought some hot dogs from a street vender and both ate well—Buddy preferred no sauerkraut—and then rested in the park grass.

We stayed in St. Augustine for the one full day. The next landfall would be Ft. Pierce, one-hundred-sixty nautical miles. There are four markers at Cape Canaveral, A through D, which warn mariners to come no closer to the Cape than 2.8 miles. They formed a semicircle around the danger zone surrounding the space shuttle activity. We set a course for marker A, hoping to get a look at the gantry and that our arrival would not coincide with a launch. With my luck the exhaust would blow us to Scotland or parts unknown.

We cleared the inlet offshore marker as a brisk and constant northerly 25-knot breeze filled both our sails. All day I read and dozed, between watching our speed and course. After a spaghetti dinner and some meaty food for Buddy, we retired for the night. I had seen no boats and the St. John River was far behind.

I woke to the proximity alarm at 3:00 a.m. and immediately saw marker A passing two-hundred feet off the starboard beam. Wow, I thought, what accuracy these modern electronics were capable of performing. I adjusted my course to 152.69°, a few degrees easterly, ten miles to marker B.

In the clear night sky, a half-moon gave light to the shoreline. The wind had settled to twenty knots, so I decided to put up the spinnaker, a parachute-like sail for running downwind or even a beam reach. I had performed this maneuver many times, but with another crewmember taking care of stern sheets so I could operate the halyard. I dug out the spinnaker bag assuming my racing buddies had packed it correctly. It seemed they had, so I proceeded

I winched up the spinnaker sail: it opened halfway up so I continued to winch with one hand and pull the furling line to douse the jenny with the other. It was a sad mess but I finally got the jenny replaced with the spinnaker. It was an exhilarating sight.

Before long we reached maker B and from there it was a straight shot to C and D back to 160° and Ft. Pierce. I had a great look at the gantry from C. We flew the spinnaker all the way to the offshore marker at the Ft. Pierce Inlet, 79.5 miles to the south.

I planned to stay a night or two with my brother, Ralph, and sister-in-law Lois, who lived on the Atlantic side of Hutchinson Island in the winter months. We had spoken some days earlier and decided I should anchor on a small lagoon at the extreme north end of the island at my estimated time of arrival.

When I arrived and anchored in the lagoon, darkness had fallen. I called Ralph to let him know I had arrived and suggested he drop over in the morning to pick up Buddy and me.

During my morning coffee and Buddy's main meal of the day, I sensed, more than heard, Ralph on the shore, trying to let me know he had arrived. In thirty minutes, we secured the boat, rowed ashore in the dinghy, and were on our way to Ralph's condominium.

Among my male siblings, Ralph alone reminds me of our dad. Dad was assertive, dogmatic, and opinionated. So were all of his sons. However, neither Dad nor Ralph ever exhibited any buffoonery, at least not in my presence. Nor did their serious assertions ever lack the perception of authority. Currie and I never really could argue with Dad *or* Ralph, without feeling we were out on a limb at the outset. The one exception was when I was manic or even hypomanic, and I had been for weeks.

After ending a one-on-one theological discussion during the visit, Ralph said to me, "You're the most arrogant son-of-a-bitch I've ever talked to!" Now that was saying something. He made this statement while proclaiming his love for me, his 'black sheep' little brother—love just like Dad had for me. Anyway, it was great to see a rational soul and my big brother who made me think of Dad.

Lois had greeted us with her immutable charm and lovely spirit. Buddy knew he did not belong in such immaculate surroundings; she gently led him to the lanai.

The short visit was great. The morning of the second day Lois opened the lanai as I slept. Buddy came charging up on me and licked me awake. I had actually slept. I felt both a great calm and very much at home. The day before, the three of us had spoken at length about many things.

As I held Buddy, the emotional force driving me to round the Florida Keys left me. I had sailed the Keys several times before, but even that familiarity gave me little comfort. I would take the safe and short route home. My hypomania was ebbing.

After saying goodbye to Ralph and his wife, we sailed 19.4 miles south in the Intracoastal Waterway before a light breeze to the mouth of the St. Lucie River, which enters the mainland as a large winding river. Motoring eleven miles further on a tight winding river took us into a twenty-one-mile, man-made canal that ended in a lock at the eastern edge of Lake Okeechobee.

The tree-lined river and canal was calm. For the first time I felt hot, and Buddy was panting a bit. However, when we entered the lock I could hear the tumult on the other side.

We rose with the waters in the lock, but only five of the available twenty feet. I should have realized at that time the Lake Okeechobee was very low. Instead, only fifty yards out, I hoisted all sails and began a broad starboard reach to the southwest. My chart had indicated the mean low water depths were from eight to thirteen feet all the way to the southern edge of the lake where I could navigate a marked channel to the lock.

The northerly wind was 20-25 knots and the lake was choppy with nasty five-foot waves. We made a lone marker #6, seven miles from the lock without difficulty, but in a matter of minutes, I was hard aground. The chart said 9.8 feet. I drew about five feet in a broad reach and I should have had a good four feet of water beneath my keel. I furled up the jenny, used the engine to turn back into the wind, and the main to heel the boat 30º—making my draft closer to four feet. I revved the engine, turned the tiller hard starboard and felt the boat slowly came about. The lake bottom seemed to be of a mud-like substance. Sand, rocks or rotting tree trunks would have made for a more difficult escape.

I scanned the scores of depths marked on the chart around my location. I noticed a privately maintained marker due west that indicated a mostly thirteen-foot depths for the entire 7.5 miles. We sailed at a beam reach, with main only, to keep a level keel.

Once we reached the non-descript marker I turned SSW for 4.5 miles to a flashing four-second green #7 marker. Our path crossed some declining depths—thirteen feet, then eleven, then nine and down to as little as three feet. We bumped a few times, but the up and down motion of the waves kept us from running hard aground. Leaving marker #7 to our port side, we entered a well-marked channel leading to the Clewiston canal, which ultimately brought us to the lock at Moore Haven, a total of twenty nautical miles

Once in the canal, both wind and sea became calmer. We cruised along peacefully at about four knots. Two hours after sunset, we arrived at the anchorage just northwest of the lock.

As Buddy and I lay in our bunk, I recollected my anxiety while crossing the lake. I knew I was coming down from an eight-month high. I was no longer even hypomanic. Although I prayed a great deal during the extremely rough times offshore, I never lost faith in *my* experience and ability to survive any incident. Now I reckoned God must have intervened at times, so I believed my mental condition had been one long delusion of grandeur.

Instead of awaking at dawn, as had been my custom, I found it hard to drag myself out of bed at 9:00 a.m. and face the day. I knew we had sixty-five miles of motoring and sailing without the tiller pilot. It would be a hands-on effort for at least ten hours before I could make the tack around Sanibel Island, across from Ft. Myers, into the open Gulf of Mexico.

If the northeasterly wind held, by nightfall we could be in an easy NNW starboard tack and a broad reach that we could maintain for a hundred miles. I could aim the autopilot accordingly, go below and sleep for eighteen hours. This would put us about sixty miles due west of our final destination.

After much needed sleep, punctuated by short lucid times, we changed course, trimmed the sails, and made for the Manatee River and our prearranged slip at Regatta Point and our new home—with a 360° waterfront.

Thirty-four – Manic Reunion

One loyal friend is worth ten thousand relatives.
Euripides

In April of 2005, after living at Regatta Point Marina in the luxury of amenities not unlike those offered by the Bradenton Yacht Club, I grew weary of the $750 monthly docking fee. So Buddy and I moved four-and-a-half miles west—to a boat yard on the south side of the mouth of the river, almost to Tampa Bay. I took the slip at the very end near the breakwater for $200 a month.

The lack of job or purpose helped move me from a hypomanic state to a full manic episode. I went on a spending spree with what was left of my credit. I bought a Yamaha V-Max 1300 motorcycle and a generator to power my A/C, and planned to move somewhere in Terra Ceia Bay, just north of the river where I could anchor for free.

For some reason I dyed my long hair and beard black and proceeded to brandish and fire my .38 in a manic mayhem. Someone called the police who used the Baker Act to place me in the hospital Psych ward. I remember the police being involved, but they didn't seize my weapon; I must have hidden it. I remember little of this stay, but I do remember being in isolation.

When the seventy-two hours of the Baker Act had expired, I attempted to get released against medical advice. I had never accomplished this before. The three days had always stretched into weeks or months. This time I tore the place up and threatened the aides. They finally released me—as manic as I was when I came in.

I recovered my pistol, packed a few things, and drove to St. Petersburg to meet my cousin Richard, twenty-six years my senior, for a ride to Tennessee and a Patton family reunion. On the ride there, my mania ebbed as I concentrated on creating a Power Point Presentation using my notebook and a scanner. Dick's calm voice added audio to pictures scanned of the family. He was our acknowledged historian with information dating back to the 1800s. He had hundreds of photographs filed neatly by the names of my grandfather's nine children, twenty-six grandchildren of whom I am the youngest, great grandchildren in the double digits, and countless great, great grandchildren—with a story for each picture. Having something to occupy my mind helped ease my mood as we drove the eight-hundred miles of two-lane roads; it was as soothing as a long Sunday drive.

The most memorable event of the reunion was a barbershop rendition of *My Wild Irish Rose* by my three siblings and me, who had no doubt received a portion of our mother's musical talent. Both the performance and the Power Point slide presentation seemed to be well received by the dozens in attendance.

In the evening, I spent my time with my favorite nephew and his wife doing Tequila shots. By the end of the reunion, the alcohol had quieted my mood down to a mild hypomanic state.

After long goodbyes and group pictures, leaving most of my relatives with the impression that the youngest grandson was either curiously eccentric or not playing with a full deck, Dick and I returned to Florida.

To continue my plan of living aboard at anchor as opposed to a slip with a monthly rent, I purchased a new nine-foot Zodiac inflatable dinghy and a 2hp Honda outboard for access to and from land. I had sunk the small wooden dinghy during bad weather a month prior and lost my secondary laptop, a riot style 12-gauge shotgun, a floodlight and almost my dog. The cell phone I lost was my seventh overboard since leaving Annapolis months before.

Buying the dinghy was the final purchase that exhausted my credit and maxed out all but two of twelve credit cards. When I had passed the one-hundred-thousand dollar unsecured credit mark, my manic mind considered it just a detail.

Apparently, my adjunct professor-status at Keiser and Everglades Universities had been dropped, I never heard from them again. I had no work, no income and little cash. David, my son-in-law, helped me launch my new dinghy and mount the outboard and agreed to let me work for him for $10/hour, an arrangement that was to be short-lived.

I tied the dinghy to the stern of my boat and made for Emerson Point, marking the north-side mouth of the Manatee River. It was a State Park; I anchored there temporarily. My sister had found a small marina in Terra Ceia Bay, where I could dock my dinghy on a daily basis for forty dollars a month. I planned to return to my boat every night. I gave my dog, Buddy, to Marie, his "mom," after realizing he should not be forced to stay on the boat all day with no dock.

After going ashore to buy cables to repel any theft, I launched the dinghy at Tropic Isles Marina. Darkness was falling and my temporary anchorage was still three miles away. Running the dinghy full throttle would take forty-five minutes to cover the distance. My final anchorage in the Bay would be less than a mile from my small slip.

Once through The Cut between the bay and the river, fog set in along with the darkness. I was probably within three hundred yards of my boat—I couldn't see it—when I ran out of gas and reached for the oars. The tide was strong coming out of the river, and I knew I'd have only one shot at reaching my boat before the tide would drag me out into Tampa Bay. When it seemed as though I'd passed my boat in the dark, I rowed hard across the tide for the unseen shore of Emerson Point.

Thirty-five – Manhunt

I know well what I am fleeing from but not what I am in search of.
Michel de Montaigne

I secured my dinghy to a mangrove limb. Only a short muck through the mangroves brought me to some picnic tables on the Point.

Four miles ESE the lights of Bradenton were beginning to shine through the lifting fog. I sat at a table and analyzed my dilemma. I could see some boats, but not mine; the lights of the city were directly behind them. I calculated the strong tide would last only about four hours. I would wait until I could easily row out to the boats and find mine.

The park was about one-and-a-half miles long and a half-mile wide; I was on the extreme western tip opposite the gate to the narrow road from one end of the park to the other. As I waited impatiently, I heard the sound of an engine coming up the road that emerged from the mangroves, ten yards from where I sat.

I walked to the road and stood in the middle. Bright headlights blocked my night vision, so I just stood and waved my hands over my head. The engine of the vehicle never slowed; it came within inches of hitting me before I jumped into the mangroves. I watched a man and a young teenage girl in an ATV make a large circular turn in the picnic area before coming directly toward me again at full throttle. Instinct or mania made me reach for my pistol. I held it high so it could be seen and was about to squeeze off a round when they abruptly skidded to a stop at my knees. I immediately concealed my weapon and explained my situation and my need for only a cupful of gasoline.

The young man declared that drawing my weapon was unnecessary—they would have stopped. I knew better: the girl was driving. Still, they seemed friendly and said they would get a ranger to help me. I stepped aside and let them by.

I returned to the picnic table and laid out my ID's and Concealed Firearms Permit. Recalling the times I had to surrender my weapon and wait a week to get it back from the sheriff or police property rooms, I decided to hide it under a dead horseshoe crab shell.

Ten minutes later a large truck with floodlights glaring stopped thirty feet away. A young man in his early twenties jumped out and aimed what looked like a .45 semi-automatic right at my chest. "Put your hands up! Do you have a gun on you?"

"Not on me," I declared honestly, as I raised my hands.

"Where is it; I know you have one?" he countered.

"I threw it in the bushes, can I please explain?" I said as I starting to walk toward him.

"Stop where you are," he ordered.

I continued to walk slowly toward the young man and dropped my hands in an attempt to defuse the situation. "My ID's are the table; I am not a criminal. I'm trying to get to my boat just off shore there." I pointed.

"Stay where you are or I swear I'll shoot you! You are being charged with trespassing on State Property," he yelled, as he chambered a round in his weapon.

I turned and walked back to the table. He would have to shoot me in the back. The encounter was manic and could have gone psychotic; I did not care at this point. Maybe his 9/11 fears and my black beard and long hair gave him the idea I was a Moslem terrorist with a Florida accent. He must have thought he had Emerson Point Park's first criminal since before he was born.

He dialed his phone but never removed me from his sight. "I am calling the Sheriff."

"Okay."

After talking and listening for a bit he put his phone away, holstered his pistol and said, "I have to open the gate for the sheriff. If you want to run, go ahead; we will find you."

The ranger turned around and sped off. I did not hesitate. I retrieved my weapon, shoved off in my dinghy, and rowed like mad for the middle of the river, where the tide would help me escape to the expanse of Tampa Bay.

After thirty minutes, I could see red and blue lights and several floodlights erratically searching the waters, trying to capture the "terrorist." The fog was lifting but I hoped I was still out of range. I quit rowing and lay down in the dinghy to become a smaller target.

Lying there, my mind was racing. I am going to jail again. No, they will just put me in the hospital. No, I'll go to court and fight it. No, I'll just wait until they're gone and the tide changes. Relax... relax; I lit a cigarette. It seemed hours were passing.

As I approached the familiar #4-range marker, I was well over a mile away from the point and the lights were gone. I had to keep from going any farther out. I knew the channel ended at this point and it was only a matter of yards west to a one-foot deep shoal; I could stick an oar in the bottom and wait for the incoming tide.

After another hour, the tide moved slowly eastward and back up the river. My mania diminished as I focused on rowing the dinghy a mile or so back to my boat. After forty-five minutes of rowing, I had little energy left. I tried the engine again thinking it would be in vain, but it started. I didn't think it would run for long. To my surprise, it took me all the way to my boat, now visible because of a makeshift dim anchor light swinging from my boom.

I became more paranoid the closer I came to the boat, both from the mood I was in and the realization they were out to get me. I boarded quickly and quietly, tied up the dinghy, started the diesel, upped the anchor and headed west to the Bay at full bore.

By the time I reached the northwest pass where the large ships enter Tampa Bay, it was dawn and blowing about 12 knots easterly, so I hoisted all sail and headed north.

All day and night, I sailed. I was not planning to stop but on the second day I thought I'd found a good place to hide—eighty miles north and then twelve more miles up the Homosassa River as far as the markers went. It was all beautiful wilderness: no people. I dropped anchor and stayed the night.

When I am manic or even hypomanic, I feel compelled to keep moving toward some allusive goal—a vague objective that continues to change undiscernibly toward increasingly fantastic proportions.

I turned back down river the next day to the Gulf of Mexico and began sailing northward again in the direction of my goal. I made it to the headwater springs of the Crystal River. I purchased some beer and water, wrote my sister concerning the problem on Emerson Point, and let her know I was heading further north every day.

By now, Emerson point was five counties and over a hundred miles to the south. I tried to relax and enjoyed snorkeling in the springs. I stayed three days.

Back in the Gulf, I made way to Cedar Key, where my ultimate goal would materialize.

Thirty-six – Haiti in My Mind

My theory has always been, that if we are to dream, the flatteries of hope are as cheap, and pleasanter, than the gloom of despair.
Thomas Jefferson

C edar Key had grown in population and construction since I was last there having dinner at a small bar and grill. It was 1965 and group of us had been hunting deer in Gulf Hammock across a rickety wooden bridge on the mainland. By the spring of 2005 it was a small tourist resort.

With my boat anchored out, I tied my dinghy to a small dock and went ashore. Somewhere in my randomly multitasking brain, I managed to focus for a moment on the fact that I had five dollars to my name. I quickly dismissed the thought as just one of many obstacles to overcome before I could realize my dream: sailing two-thousand miles to Haiti and finding a wife.

I found myself in a bar using all remaining funds to buy a couple of drafts. A well-dressed man about my age introduced himself as Jim and asked if that was my boat at anchor in sight from our barstools through a large picture window. I told him it was, and related my dream. This opened a line of questions and conversation that lasted two hours. He knew I was broke, so he started a tab for the many beers we drank during our discussion.

I explained that I was stuck here until I collected on the $360 per month loan I had made to a relative some years before. I asked him if he would like to buy a TV and twenty-some DVDs I had on the boat. He said no at first, but I think he wanted to help me.

"How about forty dollars?" I asked

"Agreed. I'll wait for you here."

"I'll be back in twenty minutes," I assured him.

After we loaded his purchases in his car, we returned to the bar to increase his tab. He told me he owned a car dealership and might be interested in buying my car if I owned one. Surely, I would need more cash to sail to Haiti. I agreed. We discussed my car and he said he could give me up to $5,000 for my six-year-old Honda CRV that was in excellent condition.

Together we went back to his car and drove to an ATM to get some cash. He gave twice what I had asked for and said this should cover the bus fare to take me back to Bradenton to get the title and my SUV. He returned me to the dock and said he would be there at seven in the morning to take me to the bus stop in Chiefland.

My beer-soaked brain had little effect on my manic dreaming. By 2:00 a.m., I was sitting on a lifeguard tower practicing my French Creole aloud to moonlight. Confident I'd have sufficient money for the voyage, I just knew it was all going to take place as I'd foreseen. I would make landfall at Cozumel in Mexico, Montego Bay in Jamaica and finally, Les Cayes, Haiti.

Jim picked me up as planned and I was at my sister's in Bradenton by nightfall. I intended to get the title from my files that permanently resided at her house. The long bus ride had mellowed my extreme mood and when I tried to sleep on Patty's couch, realism attacked my dream.

Patty had been at the dock a week or so before when I launched my dinghy with the idea of getting to my boat and sailing it around Emerson Point to a permanent anchorage in Terra Ceia Bay. She had received my letter detailing my problems with the police. Now she was angry and told me what a stupid idea I had and that the sheriff couldn't possibly know who or where I was. She had no doubt that I could sail to Haiti, but that I knew good and well it had become a police state since I was last there.

I wanted to argue, but Patty was livid. I had hoped she would bless my trip—glad to be rid of me for a long time. She reminded me I had promised to work helping David with his business.

I had medication to mitigate my mania, but rarely used it. I knew I had reached the point of panic between my mania and psychotic states: I took a handful of clonazepam. My exciting dream, vivid and detailed as those in my sleep, slowly came apart as my mind grasped the dull reality of my existence.

I finally agreed to let David drive me back to Cedar Key to get my boat. It was 3:00 a.m. when I got underway and began a three-day non-stop sail back home to the spot I had chosen in Terra Ceia Bay to anchor and live. I didn't have an opportunity to get in touch with Jim.

Thirty-seven – Hard Labor

They say hard work never hurt anybody, but I figure why take the chance.
Ronald Reagan

My new routine was to be up by 6:30 a.m., prepare my coffee, ready the dinghy, and motor the half-mile to my tiny docking space in the marina. I walked to my car three blocks away and then drove seven miles to David and Veronica's home, arriving by eight. After a full day's work I reversed the routine, arriving back at my boat with water and other supplies.

David's company specialized in pool deck finishing—with pebble, rubber, pavers and other decking materials. About once a week we would completely redo the Marcite and retile a pool, as well as refinish the deck. At first, I could only do unskilled labor: carry numerous hundred-pound bags of concrete, and the fifty-pound bags of rubber, pebble and mix for David to trowel. Eventually I became adept at grinding Marcite, placing and grouting tile, and other finishing tasks.

Every morning, for a year-and-a-half, I hated getting up to face work. I was an academic, a paper-pusher and had never done manual tasks for very long. However, by the time I'd had my coffee and watched the sunrise paint the sky on the glassy waters as I cruised in my dinghy, my mood changed. When I met up with David, with his delightful attitude and easy personality, I experienced true joy and anticipation. What were we going to do today?

By day's end, I felt great and ready to motor back to my boat, usually in the dark. Often choppy waves came over my bow soaking me through. Seldom did I ever waste water on my boat for showering.

Hard physical work in the heat or, on rare occasions, cold, acted like medicine for my depression. Saturdays I attended the Seventh Day Adventist church and Sundays I went to either the Church of the Cross or Christ Episcopal. After church on these days, I would find someone to visit or take my lady friends, Sunny, or Mary, out for dinner and a show. I rode out many storms at anchor, but not Hurricane Charlie. I battened down the hatches and watched my boat from shore. It never broke anchor and no damage occurred even though the eye of the hurricane passed just to the south, surrounded by 140 mph winds. Boats docked ashore were less fortunate: damage there was the rule.

In early September 2005, I joined a team that caravanned to New Orleans to help with the havoc left by Hurricane Katrina. For two weeks, I felt positive and energized as I came to know and work with the people from different church denominations. The scene of destruction was horrible to behold. I was thankful for what I had, little as it seemed before this trip.

The remainder of 2005 and most of the next year, I worked with David. Sometimes our jobs were out-of-town projects that took several days to complete. I enjoyed the long rides when David and I could just talk. His spirit brought profound peace to my soul. He is a good man and husband to my daughter.

By the fall of 2006, we were spending an increasing amount of time working on separate jobs, each in our own area. In early October, I shifted to a hypomanic mood as I accomplished more and more with increasing quality in my work. This was the first time in a year-and-a-half that I began to move from my normal mood, with only intermittent periods of depression. I experienced a wonderful, but short-lived change.

Joy and aspiration returned, but without medication, it soon turned to mania. Even David was upset with my swing from euphoric to sometimes-irritable moods, and eventually outright madness and frenzy.

I do not remember the details but somehow, with psychosis seeming inevitable, I apparently made trouble at the hospital ER in an effort to get some meds. The police arrived to arrest me by force. One ER doctor successfully argued that they should take me to the psychiatric hospital, rather than jail. They provided the usual treatment; talk therapy, drug adjustment and observation.

The doctor released me after a two-week stay; I was still experiencing a mild hypomanic state. The one drug I had taken consistently for twelve years was clonazepam, or Klonopin, a strong benzodiazepine. It works by decreasing abnormal electrical activity in the brain. It treats high anxiety, panic attack, and convulsions, and sometimes manic-depressive psychosis. The *Physicians' Desk Reference* shows no study of long-term use and warns against it. However, the literature does caution that sudden withdrawal can be fatal. I have gone from an Rx dose of one tablet per day to six, and even eight, per day. I have often taken significantly larger single doses to relieve severe mania, paranoia and panic attacks.

The drugs I took with me, as an outpatient this time, for some reason, did not include clonazepam.

Thirty-eight – Withdrawal

Panic is a sudden desertion of us, and a going over
to the enemy of our imagination.
Christian Nestell Bovee

Newly released from the psychiatric hospital, I climbed in my car and started driving toward St. Petersburg. Driving has a calming effect on me. Nonetheless, my withdrawal came swiftly. I drove all over the city from 10 a.m. to dawn the next day.

I found myself in the oncoming traffic lane of a large convoluted Interstate #275 interchange. After barely escaping a head-on collision, I pulled off on the shoulder. My night of driving around with horrifying thoughts and waking nightmare-imaginings spinning in my head had taken its toll. I dialed 911 on my cell. I was powerless to articulate my actual situation, but I did get my position known.

In minutes, two police cars, a sheriff deputy, a fire engine and an ambulance appeared—apparently due to the vagueness of the situation. I tried to answer all their questions, but was unsuccessful. They put me in the paramedic's truck then shortly decided to move me to a cop car. All manner of thoughts assaulted my mind.

Ultimately, the police took me to a mental facility. It became obvious this warehouse-like building housed drug addicts, criminals, derelicts, homeless and perhaps, a few mental patients; it was enormously crowded and nothing resembling any other mental ward I had frequented with the exception of the State Mental Hospital.

I became exceedingly agoraphobic when standing in lines, eating in a cramped fifteen-by-fifteen square-foot cafeteria, and going out to smoke in a group. I feared I was out of control. Help seemed impossible to obtain, invoking a periodic fight-or-flight response.

I could not sleep in a room with two other patients. I would lie still for fifteen minutes, and then walk out into the warehouse; the sole aide on watch would see me and become gradually angrier as I repeated this process all night. In the daytime, I would return to bed quickly.

Each day seemed worse than the last. Then after a week or so had passed, an angel appeared at the only door to the outside—it was my sister Patty. Her husband Bob was with her. My perception was that her visit calmed me and was a high point. Later Patty related to me that I had taken tiny, stiff, robotic steps. She could see fear and desperation in my puffy red eyes and, and my conversation was unintelligible. She left crying.

All feeling of calmness left with her, and my mental situation deteriorated even more than before the visit. There was no hope, there never had been. I was in a timeless existence that would continue eternally—like Hell. I preferred suffering physical pain—and death would have been welcome at any given moment.

I have trouble remembering that nothing lasts forever, at least so far in my life. At times, my brain, mind and emotions become self-destructive instruments; the Spirit, conversely, whispers a quickly vanishing yet persistent hope. Two more weeks went by before Pat returned to take me home. What was it, the fifteenth or twentieth time? I have never counted.

A laboriously typewritten letter to the outpatient office and to my East Indian Psychiatrist, whom I visited every three months, resulted in an immediate prescription for clonazepam. After three days on the medication, I was almost myself—hypomanic, but normal otherwise.

Several days after release, I tried to repeat the driving exercise. Whatever drugs the St. Petersburg clinic had treated me with in mid-November of 2006 had no effect on my manic brain. I went by to see my brother Currie, but it resulted in a quick getaway on my part. I do not remember the essence of our short visit.

I returned to Bradenton about 8:00 p.m. full of clonazepam but out of gas. My mind was reeling from lack of sleep over the past four weeks, when I saw a friendly face walking her friendly dog.

It was my special former sister-in-law, Sue Ann. She knew of my illness from Marie, my ex-wife yet soul mate, and knew I was having trouble. Sue Ann told me to park in her driveway and wait for her. We sat on the porch and I tried to articulate my problem. She went in and called Marie. Within fifteen minutes, she arrived and tried to join the conversation. With both of them healthcare professionals, it was easy to agree to let them take me to the emergency room. They stayed for hours, waiting for me to respond to sleep treatment.

Finally, they told me they wanted to admit me to the psychiatric ward. I had no fear or panic, just mania from lack of sleep.

Thirty-nine – Peace

This happiness consisted of nothing else but the harmony of the few
things around me with my own existence, a feeling of contentment
and well-being that needed no changes and no intensification.
Herman Hesse

D r. X, a new psychiatrist born in the Dominican Republic and
educated by Jesuit Priests prior to medical school, became my
physician and mentor. He met with me at least once and often twice a
day while I was confined in the psychiatric hospital for about eight weeks
including Christmas and New Year's.

His obvious concern, gentle demeanor, and genuine desire to listen and
understand, slowly brought me to a rational acceptance of my illness and
my need for a few drugs. His manner was the exception to the rule among
the numerous other psychiatrists who had treated me.

By Christmas, I was able to join in the festivities of the ward, but a
day or so later, my sleeplessness brought on a convulsion. An ambulance
rushed me to the emergency room a few miles away. By the time I came
around, the ER doctor had prescribed medication and placed me in a sleep
unit. The next day they returned me to the ward where Dr. X explained
my critical need for sleep.

He related that long-term sleep deprivation has caused death in lab
animals and humans. He suggested lying in bed hoping for at least some

micro sleep. Failing at that, he started me on a high dose of an antipsychotic drug that I still take to this day. I fall asleep within an hour and sleep for up to twelve hours. I use a low dose regularly. The drug's effects also help keep my mania in check.

I began to sleep eight to ten hours every night. After eight weeks, they released me with instructions to return for a session with Dr. X a week later.

In that week, along with other manic behavior, I wrote a $15,400 check to trade in my SUV for a Jeep Wrangler. There had not been any significant funds in my account for some time. I drove to Ralph and Lois's home across the state, arriving in the very early hours of the morning. From our brief conversation, Ralph knew immediately that I was acting crazy; he had every right to be angry. He gave me fifty-dollars for gas and told me to drive straight home and seek some help.

I drove to my weekly appointment with Dr. X in my new Jeep. Somehow, he had learned of my behavior from anyone of several people. This time it was not just a session but also a new admittance to the ward that lasted another four weeks. Patty had found out what I had done and in her inimitable way managed to return the Jeep and get my car back—as well as the bad check.

Ralph came to visit me while I was in the ward—a three-hour drive from the east coast. "This is your last chance," was the crux of what I remember him saying. At the time, I was not sure exactly what he meant. I discovered later that, along with my son Sebastian, Ralph had paid several months' rent to Helen, now my landlady from whom I had been renting a bedroom, with bath and kitchen privileges. I then deduced the meaning of Ralph's statement: No more help meant, "physician heal thyself."

Dr. X accumulated all my records for the mid-1970s to date, February 2007. He presented a solid case for incurable mental illness to Social Security officials and set up an interview with them, my sister, Patty, a psychiatric nurse practitioner, and myself. This effort was successful in getting substantial monthly disability checks paid through my sister, as though I were already retired.

While I still owned a car, my small newly rented bedroom became my monastic cell. The security of knowing I had funds for living expenses was calming. My cell consisted of a bed, table and chair, but unlike a real monastery, I also had a TV, phone and laptop. Now I required focus—a project, an extensive one.

After a three or four day internet search for good accredited online schools and consideration of various subject areas, I found one that seemed promising. My B.S. in Mathematics, followed by my Masters, had been long since been achieved—on the heels of my first manic episode that resulted in my hospitalization in 1976. Newburgh Theological Seminary received my transcripts and agreed to let me enter their doctoral program. I would make tuition payments over the course of the three-year program.

My goal was not to seek a job, but to learn more of a subject about which I had little understanding. Seeking this knowledge gave me a reason to get up and face a full eight-to-ten-hour day of studying.

In a period of almost three years, I read over a hundred books, viewed more than a five hundred lectures, wrote scores of papers, and finally a dissertation with 162 references. The sense of accomplishment was settling to my illness. Theology, accompanied by theistic and atheistic philosophy, wasn't included in my mathematics background. Nevertheless, I found a great deal of logic and rationalism in theology. My rational mind opened itself to the Christian faith in a way I never imagined. The emotional aspect of my illness—and emotion in general—became my major interest, the dynamics of which provided the thesis for my dissertation.

In November 2009, my dissertation was accepted and shortly thereafter, I received my Doctor of Theology degree. I realize how much more there is for me to learn. Nonetheless, I now perceive and control my emotional illness by a more rational and spiritual thought process, assisted by medication. I continue to study and write to keep my mind active and my emotions held in check.

Part Five -
Pathways Toward the Light

With no known cure for bipolar disorder or manic-depressive illness, I had to search for ways to live with it. I could not have survived without finding sources to give me hope during my darkest hours. In Part Five I offer six paths that help me keep going, with the belief that every sufferer will prioritize what will be the most helpful for him or her.

Chapter Forty – Learn to Become Your Own Advocate

The option of solicitor advocacy came on the scene a bit too late for me.
Len G. Murray

U*nderstand your Illness:*
Gather as much information as you can about the stages of the disease and the symptoms typically associated with each stage.

Depression, in my experience, manifests itself in persistent feelings of sadness, anxiety and guilt. I can't concentrate. Sometimes I am irritable or even angry at the world and anyone around me. When I become shy or suffer social anxiety I feel isolated and lonely. I lose interest in activities I once enjoyed, including sex. I am indifferent and have no motivation. Why would I? Everything seems hopeless.

At times I suffer severe bipolar depression and endure psychotic symptoms—including visions, delusions, hallucinations and even memory loss. I entertain thoughts of suicide and twice acted on those thoughts. To ameliorate these feelings, I turn to large amounts of caffeine, and my prescription drugs.

Sometimes I experience a heightened self-awareness and feel I am watching myself act, but have no control over what is happening. The world seems less real, a very disturbing experience. This leads to severe anxiety and when these feelings become most intense, panic attacks plague me. I often feel I am living in a nightmare.

Many times over the years, particularly after each hospitalization for mania, great doses of tranquilizers have been given to me, which always triggered depression. Again I face the symptoms and feel the timelessness that accompanies the complete lack of hope. "How long wilt thou forget me, O LORD? Forever?"

When I'm in a depression the most minor tasks seem insurmountable, my personal hygiene becomes almost absent, and sleep is the only escape. It has been spiritually and emotionally contagious to those around me, and often caused a lesser form of the same symptoms in my loved ones. Your wife, girlfriend, or relatives might not be frightened by your clinical depression (not the "blues"), but, like mine, they judge you as lazy or slovenly.

Hypomania is experienced as a continuum from depression toward mania, with no clear distinction between levels. During this phase I cannot escape my elevated mood. I have little need for rest or sleep and have a great deal of energy. I become extremely outgoing and competitive. I am fully functional and often astonishingly more productive than usual. I seek this state as often as possible; I find it intoxicating and addicting. I skip some meds and increase others to move from the debilitating state of depression to my productive stage of hypomania.

Being hypomanic can be compared to doing a three-hundred-dollar-a-day "eight ball" of cocaine during an eighteen-hour workday. Cocaine is a powerful nervous system stimulant that increases one's alertness, sense of well-being, and euphoria. Energy and motor activity rev up, as do the feelings of competence and sexuality. Cocaine is a strong serotonin-norepinephrine and primarily dopamine reuptake inhibitor. It is one strong antidepressant, but dangerous for all of us and devastating to the manic. Even without the drug, dopamine flows and sufferers of manic-depressive psychosis feel extraordinarily confident, albeit not yet able to leap tall buildings. Progression to the manic stage makes all seem possible.

As my mood proceeds higher and higher toward a manic state, it has the effect of a drug, not unlike methamphetamine, a psychoactive stimulant. Add a hallucinogenic, such as "acid," and manic psychosis follows. These illegal drugs must be avoided; the resulting highs are much more elevated than expected and appropriate medications are forgotten. Treatment in a psych ward is inevitable and the crash afterward is worse than you would think possible.

The symptoms in the hypomanic phase help me perform my job with great quality and efficiency. I have no desire to come down. As long as my mood doesn't get too high, people are pleased to have me around and are taken in by my charm and apparent intelligence. Somewhere on the continuum between the bi-polar extremes is my "normal." Most of my life I've tried to maintain this state, often by altering my medications. The move to a manic state is inevitable—although sometimes it takes months.

Mania, for me, varies in intensity, from mild mania, or high hypomania, to full-scale mania with psychotic attributes, including hallucinations and delusions. Some of my symptoms go unnoticed by me at the time, but I'm aware of the feelings of euphoria, hyper-sexuality, and grandiosity. My speech is more rapid as I try to keep up with my racing thoughts, and I have no need for sleep. The drive toward self-selected, goal-directed activities is uncontrollable.

Sleep deprivation exacerbates my mania as I go more and more days and nights without sleep. A 1999 study found that sleep deprivation results in reduced cortisol secretion the very next day, driven by increased subsequent slow-wave sleep. Sleep deprivation has been found to enhance activity on the hypothalamic-pituitary-adrenal axis (which controls reactions to stress and regulates body functions such as digestion, the immune system, *mood*, sex, or energy usage). (Vgontzas AN, Mastorakos G, Bixler EO, Kales A, Gold PW, Chrousos GP (August 1999). *[Emphasis added]*.

Worse yet, "The specific causal relationships between sleep loss and effects on psychiatric disorders have been most extensively studied in patients with mood disorders. Shifts into mania in bipolar patients are often preceded by periods of insomnia, and sleep deprivation has been shown to induce a manic state in susceptible individuals. Sleep deprivation may represent a final common pathway in the genesis of mania, and sleep loss is both a precipitating and reinforcing factor. *For more extensive information see:http://en.wikipedia.org/wiki/Sleep_deprivation#Effects_on_the_brain.*

In full mania I often feel as though my goals are more important than all else. I spend money I don't have. I drive miles to see a relative, arriving at all hours, because I lose my ability to discern day or night. If my car runs out of gas, I walk miles. There appears no need to exercise restraint in pursuing my objective, because I am convinced negative consequences, if any, would be minimal. Being somewhat intelligent, I adopt seemingly genius characteristics and my ability to perform and articulate thoughts go far beyond normal.

At the extreme end of this mood, I am unequivocally dangerous. I do possess a concealed firearms permit, but no longer own a weapon. People around me often find my speech difficult to understand and they rightly become fearful. If I do not check myself into a psych ward, someone else will—unless the police put me in a cell first. A complete psychotic state is inevitable for me after six to eleven days of no sleep. Even a perceived attack from an encounter with the police initiates my fight or flight response.

The depressed side of manic depression is by far the worst for the sufferer. It is, however the easiest for family and friends to bear, although they usually view it as a character flaw.

Kay Redfield Jamison, a clinical psychiatrist and writer, is considered the foremost expert on bipolar disorder. Since early childhood she has been a sufferer herself. Currently she holds the position of Professor of Psychiatry at the Johns Hopkins University School of Medicine. In her book she abridges the entire cycle of manic-depression.

> "Which of the me's is me? The wild, impulsive, chaotic, energetic and crazy one? Or the shy, withdrawn, desperate, suicidal one? Probably a bit of both, hopefully much that is neither." (Kay Redfield Jamison, *An Unquiet Mind – A*

Memoir of Moods and Madness, Random House, Inc. 1745 Broadway, New York, NY 10036, (1995): 67, 68.)

Dr. Jamison's book is, by far, the most articulate, informative, and helpful book on the market. I recommend it highly for sufferers of this insidious disease.

Know Your Physician and Medications:

Find a compassionate physician you trust, have confidence in, and feel comfortable with. Learn about the medications prescribed for you. Many psychiatrists have treated me over the course of my life; two were good, the rest, poor. Keep searching until you find a doctor you are comfortable with. If any become offended when you leave their care, it should not be your concern.

If you have the ability to afford a private psychiatrist you will likely have more, if not immediate access. I am able to schedule only quarterly visits. In federally funded hospitals or outpatient clinics where I receive my care, foreign doctors are permitted to practice without a state license. The accents of the doctors make them difficult to understand, and they in turn, find it difficult to understand me or have any compassion for my misery.

The five-minute, unintelligible interviews result in my receiving the same medication prescribed three months previously. Some insist on lengthy psychoanalysis, having nothing to do with my chemical, neurological illness. I am left with a seventy-five or a hundred-dollar bill for each weekly visit

Manic-depressive illness is a fluctuating phenomenon that requires at least monthly reassessment. Only in the confines of a hospital, is daily observation possible. But drugs can lose their effectiveness and some I cannot tolerate. So dosage, if not certain prescriptions, must be changed promptly. If I cannot reach my psychiatrist to get what I need when I need it, I don't hesitate to request a change of doctors.

My medications are vital for the management of my illness, so I want to know as much about them as I possibly can. I always read the information provided by the pharmacist with any new prescription. I refer to the PDR (*Physician's Desk Reference,*) the *Merck Manual of Diagnosis and Therapy,* or research what is available on the internet. I am not afraid to tell my doctor what I think about a drug and then ask him to explain or correct me. If it is not doing the job, I want something else. I have learned to be my own advocate.

Chapter Forty-one –
Commit to A Twelve-Step Program

Twelve significant photographs in any one year is a good crop.
Ansel Adams

Twelve–step programs have been adopted to address a wide range of issues, such as substance abuse, dependency issues, and mental health problems. Over two-hundred organizations—often known as fellowships—with a worldwide membership of millions, now employ twelve-step principles for recovery. God, or a higher power, figures highly in the healing of the sufferer.

Bill Wilson and Dr. Bob Smith founded the first twelve-step fellowship, Alcoholics Anonymous (AA), in Akron, Ohio in 1935. Members knew them as Bill W. and Dr. Bob. A great many people who follow this program religiously have found it effective. I attended many AA fellowship meetings with a fiancé in the late '70s and have found these principles to be just as pertinent to mental health issues.

Each member states what step he or she is working on, what success or difficulties are being encountered, and receives comments from the fellowship. One can attempt to do this in private, but the help and support received from the others in the group is more valuable. Each step is a goal toward healing.

Step One: We admitted we are powerless over mental illness—that our lives have become unmanageable. As a bipolar, manic-depressive, I have no problem admitting this; it is obvious.

Step Two: Came to believe that a power greater than ourselves could restore us to sanity. If I acknowledge I am powerless, I must believe, or at least hope, there is a power greater than myself.

Step Three: Made a decision to turn our will and our lives over to the care of God, as we understand Him. For me the higher power *is* God.

Step Four: Made a searching and fearless moral inventory of ourselves. When I was depressed and suffering from guilt feelings, real or imagined, I did not find this step very helpful. When in a hypo- or manic state, I never felt guilty nor in need of judgment. When I was stabilized, step four *did* help me realistically assess my shortcomings—which is essential to address the remaining steps.

Step Five: Admitted to God, to ourselves, and to another human being the exact nature of our wrongs. As Daniel Webster said, "There is no refuge from confession but suicide: And suicide is confession." Having a fellowship "brother" or "sister" was most helpful.

Step Six: Were entirely ready to have God remove all these defects of character.

Step Seven: Humbly asked Him to remove our shortcomings. Though God may already know, it is good to include Him beforehand so steps six and seven are possible.

Step Eight: Made a list of all persons we had harmed, and became willing to make amends to them all.

Step Nine: Made direct amends to such people wherever possible, except when to do so would injure them or others.

Steps eight and nine are touchy for manic-depressives. Most people do not understand our illness. Rather, it appears as an excuse for bad character. Often I was not aware of what I had done. I decided to ask forgiveness where I thought it due, and left the results to God. In any case, making amends is instrumental in removing some *real* guilt and helps recognize *false* guilt experienced during times of depression.

Step Ten: Continued to take personal inventory and when we were wrong promptly admitted it. When I am capable, I admit my wrongs immediately.

Step Eleven: Sought through prayer and meditation to improve our conscious contact with God as we understood Him, praying only for knowledge of His will for us and the power to carry that out.

Step Twelve: Having had a spiritual awakening as the result of these steps, we tried to carry this message to those with mental illness and practice the principles in all our affairs.

Steps eleven and twelve are entirely spiritual in nature. I believe a personal link with God, our higher power, results in a binding and present reasoning that helps guide us through the *dark sides* of our illness.

Chapter Forty-two – Embrace a Spiritual Life

*Spiritual relationship is far more precious than physical. Physical
relationship divorced from spiritual is body without soul.*
Mohandas Gandhi

I recognize the Judeo-Christian God as my higher power. While not religious in the traditional sense, I am a Christian. I've heard it said, "Religion is man's attempt to reach God; Christianity is God's attempt to reach man."

God called me out of my extreme misery many years ago, giving me grace, faith, justification, and trust in Christ Jesus. While many tests of my faith have punctuated my life since then, I would be remiss if I did not mention the positive effects my faith has had on my illness. I've learned the patience required to get through the long-suffering of the dark times. I read and reread the Book of Job. He suffered greatly during his overwhelming trials, yet wrote, "Though He slay me, yet will I trust in Him." Job 13:15.

Meditation on my God occasionally takes me into the transcendent—beyond the natural. This requires focus and trust. Without meditation, my life would have been much more horrifying. Without Christ, I would long-since have disappeared into the Abyss.

I find comfort in reading the Bible. For example, Psalm 13: which is King David's prayer—with the lament of depression of the righteous.

"How long wilt thou forget me, O LORD? Forever?
How long wilt thou hide thy face from me?
How long shall I take counsel in my soul,
Having sorrow in my heart daily?
How long shall mine enemy be exalted over me?
Consider and hear me, O LORD my God:
Lighten mine eyes, lest I sleep the sleep of death:
Let mine enemy say, I have prevailed against him;
And those that trouble me rejoice when I am moved.
But I have trusted in thy mercy;
My heart shall rejoice in thy salvation. I will sing
Unto the LORD, because he hath dealt bountifully with me.

The third and fourth lines are signs of severe depression, the dark night of the soul. In spite of God's apparent absence, David chooses to sing to Him in faith. Even before killing Goliath, King David was testified by the Lord Himself to be, "A man after God's own heart."

But without faith it is impossible to please him:
for he that cometh to God must believe that He is,
and that He is a rewarder
of them that diligently seek Him." Hebrews 11:6.

I turn also to other sources to probe the belief in a higher power:

Blaise Pascal, the brilliant French philosopher, mathematician and physicist, made a famous wager in his work *Pensées,* which in essence put forward the idea that though the existence of God cannot be determined through reason, a person should wager as though God exists— because living life accordingly has everything to gain, and nothing to lose. Pascal formulated his wager on the goodness and mercy of the Judeo-Christian God.

Albert Einstein wrote, "My religion consists of a humble admiration of the illimitable superior spirit, who reveals himself in the slight details we are able to perceive with our frail and feeble mind."

C.S. Lewis taught at Oxford for thirty years, and later was the first Professor and Fellow of Medieval and Renaissance English at the University of Cambridge. He was quoted as saying, "A man can no more diminish God's glory by refusing to worship him than a lunatic can put out the sun by scribbling the word 'darkness' on the walls of his cell."

Soren Kierkegaard wrote, "God creates out of nothing. Wonderful, you say. Yes, to be sure, but he does what is still more wonderful: he makes saints out of sinners."

Many other intelligent, productive people could be added to this list: many who do and many who do not believe in the existence of God. They may find their higher power to be science, themselves, or perhaps a cosmic force, in my opinion a temporal benefit at best.

When I speak with others suffering from manic-depressive illness and trying to fight the effects, it is clear we need something beyond ourselves to believe in—a hope for something worthy to look forward to after this difficult and miserable life. This could well be nothingness, perhaps a welcome state to some bipolar men or women. Eternal Life as promised in the Bible would be infinitely better.

A well known character compares life to suicide, but the question remains:

> "To be, or not to be: that is the question:
> Whether 'tis nobler in the mind to suffer
> The slings and arrows of outrageous fortune,
> Or to take arms against a sea of troubles,
> And by opposing *end them*? To die: to sleep;
> No more; and by a sleep to say we end
> The heart-ache and the thousand natural shocks
> That flesh is heir to, 'tis a consummation
> Devoutly to be wish'd. To die, to sleep;
> To sleep: perchance to dream: ay, there's the rub;
> For in that sleep of death what dreams may come"...*???*
> William Shakespeare - Hamlet 3/1 *[emphasis mine]*

My Christian faith offers me hope for the hereafter. I believe in Providence and a Benevolent God, who is using my illness for His purpose.

"For the Lord disciplines the one he loves, and
chastises every son whom he receives."
Hebrews 12:6

The fellowship of the Spirit is, for me, a blessing during the ins and outs of my moods of madness and depression. Without real purpose, we spend our lives in the pursuit of our desires—pleasurable, noble and/or evil. In a wisdom book of the Bible, it proposes,

"Sorrow is better than laughter; for by the sadness of the countenance the
heart is made better. The heart of the wise is in the house of mourning;
but the heart of fools is in the house of mirth....
Better is the end of a thing than the beginning thereof;
a patient in spirit is better than the proud in spirit." Ecclesiastes 7:3,4,8

Our mind can conceive horrible thoughts from our emotional illness and permanent insanity may result. Conversely, we can meditate on hope, faith and love, leading to a sound mind—rather than having our minds take us prisoner for life.

"Whatever man conceives in his mind will not be impossible unto him."
Genesis 11:6

I have encountered many people with the same positive mind set. I met my support group after a lengthy search for a church compatible with my theology. In the fellowship of the church I found several people who were either loved ones of bipolar sufferers or had the illness themselves.

While it may be difficult to find a church you feel comfortable in, I recommend searching until you do. Most non-denominational churches focus on live, contemporary music for much of the service, which could positively stir your emotions. Seek out the pastor after the service; look for one who impresses you as being friendly and positive.

Most churches have home fellowship groups. Their small size makes them easier to approach if you are experiencing any social anxiety. Don't be discouraged. If you feel uncomfortable, you can leave and try another group or even try another church.

Consider also, the public health services available in most towns or cities. Information about National Institute of Mental Health bipolar meetings should be available. If searching on your own, go to http://www.nimh.nih.gov/health/topics/bipolar-disorder/index.shtml, on the World-Wide-Web at the *Outreach* link

Chapter Forty-three – Turn to Music to Calm Your Soul

*Music is an agreeable harmony for the honor of God
and the permissible delights of the soul.*
Johannes Sebastian Bach

Meditation is difficult with a mind in turmoil. I seek transcendent music—music that takes me above mind and emotions—where my spirit exists.

The internet is replete with entries of the famous experiment to determine if music affected plant growth. The result reported most frequently determined plants *do* respond; they respond well to some music and poorly to others.

The successful methodology consisted of placing speakers in three separate greenhouses with several of the same types of plants. Group One received four hours of classical music, such as Bach, Mozart, Handel, Debussy, Beethoven, and others.

Group Two received four hours of hard-driving rock music or heavy metal, such as Slip Knot, My Chemical Romance, Linkin' Park, AC/DC, and Queen. Group Three was the control group: No music played. All other variables were held equal. Group One showed slightly greater growth than the no-music control group, and exceptionally more growth than Group Three exposed to the rock treatment.

It is my conviction these results may be so manifest because God inspires some composers. Some actually wrote music for the Church. The great composer, Johann Sebastian Bach signed each one of his masterpieces "SDG"—*Soli Deo Gloria,* or "To God alone be the glory."

In the summer of 1741, Handel, depressed and in debt, wrote the *"Messiah"* in just twenty-four days. Forty-three parts to the Oratorio and almost three hours of stimulating composition: Did he move from depression to mania, or did God inspire him?

On occasion, I do enjoy listening to rock, secular, and contemporary Christian music, but to find peace approaching the supernatural, I prefer the ethereal, eternal transcendence in the music of Bach and others like him.

This music brings peace to my soul as I meditate and contemplate eternity and the infinite. I sense a presence; my mood is both one of fear and ecstasy, similar to what one may experience entering a great cathedral. The closer I get to my Heavenly Father, the greater the reverence and ecstasy.

"Music is the art of the prophets and the gift of God," said Martin Luther. He also wrote, "Whatever your heart clings to and confides in, that is really your God."

"Finally, brothers, whatever is true, whatever is honorable, whatever is just, whatever is pure, whatever is lovely, whatever is commendable, if there is any excellence, if there is anything worthy of praise, think about these things." Philippians 4:8

Chapter Forty-four – Let Others Know How They Can Help

It is necessary to help others, not only in our prayers, but in our daily lives. If we find we cannot help others, the least we can do is to desist from harming them.
Dalai Lama

The needs of a quadriplegic are obvious: constant physical assistance and care. Family members and caretakers seemingly have no reservations in providing whatever their loved one requires. Likewise, the family of those suffering from Alzheimer's disease often tolerate years of the increasing debilitation before giving in to the alternative—institutionalization of the patient.

The response of family and friends to those suffering from manic-depression often fail to recognize the needs of those of us with this illness; our limbs are intact and we don't appear sick, even though some of our frustrating symptoms resemble those of Alzheimer's.

Our symptoms come and go and hospitalization is usually relatively short, but we need the help of those who love us. Unfortunately for some, that help may not be forthcoming—often because our illness is not understood or we have done something—perhaps unknowingly—that caused hurt and alienation.

Let friends and loved ones know how they can help us. Ask them to learn all they can about manic-depression. Perhaps something on these pages will help in that endeavor. Once they have a basic understanding, they can concentrate on the periodic good moods of our illness, and get through the exasperating ups and downs of our bad times with a heavy dose of patience, love and compassion. Regardless of how our illness affects family and friends, we are suffering far more.

When behavior can no longer be tolerated, caring family or friends should insist their loved one be admitted to a hospital or crisis stabilization unit and if necessary, have him or her committed. This offers a temporary respite and peace for caregivers. If the sufferer is asked to leave, or is disowned, divorced, or abandoned, the emotional security and essential support system are gone. Just having the presence of loved ones is extremely comforting. Once banned from this sanctuary, my illness always became worse and ultimately resulted in hospitalization.

Chapter Forty-five – Strive for a Healthy Life Style

Healthy citizens are the greatest asset any country can have.
Winston Churchill

I know it is up to me to follow this path. At times I am successful; too often I stray.

When in a long-term, relatively consistent yet manageable depressed state, I awaken after twelve hours sleep in fear of deepening depression as a result of vivid dreams, probably due to the atypical antipsychotic I took the previous night. Before I go to bed, I sometimes write myself large notes about my current condition—where I am between depression and hypomania.

Many people probably experience a mild depressed feeling for a short time after they awaken. Few, I think, always jump out of bed immediately happy to face the day.

Although I have to force myself awake after coming out of the blessed sleep when I am depressed, I've learned that it's important to get out of bed early. I have my first cigarette after awakening in the morning (something I wish I could get away from)—after meditation and before medication. Nicotine is a stimulant and a mild dopamine producer, the most effective virtue—and curse—of cocaine. Iced water and hot coffee come next. Both are probably not good on an empty stomach, not unlike oral medication. This morning pattern is not repeated when I am manic.

I take my medication— a varying amount proportionate to the rate I am improving and then, one to two hours after waking up, am I ready to begin studying, writing, or whatever the day holds for me. Succumbing to extended sleeping or lethargic activities such as watching mindless television are psychological downers and unhealthy. When I disregard this, I pay the price.

Exercise is important, of course. Long walks are helpful when I don't have access to a gym or more formal methods. Having a dog is good for me: it gets me out on walks and provides companionship and affection. I've learned that weight gain is inevitable when I am on the depressed end of the spectrum, so exercise is especially important. Paradoxically, when I am hypo-manic and more likely to exercise, my appetite decreases and I lose weight without trying.

That one's mental state affects eating habits is well understood. When I am depressed, avoiding the "wrong" foods becomes more difficult. When hypomanic I can find it hard to make the effort to eat well, because my appetite diminishes. Those of us with this illness have as great a need for healthy, nutritious food as anyone. Good health is a goal for all of us, but is essential for a manic-depressive to stay on the path toward the light.

Epilogue

Emancipate yourselves from mental slavery, none but ourselves can free our minds! One good thing about music, when it hits you, you feel no pain. Don't Worry, be Happy.
Bob Marley

I savor the good in each day. Using my mind, music and spiritual practices helps me regenerate my soul and manage even the occasional manic state.

Over the past few years, I've learned to accept mild depression, but am most comfortable when mania ebbs to a tolerable hypomania.

I have a place to live on my own and the peace of not having to speak with anyone other than my small dog, Kirby, unless I entertain the occasional visitor. My children and their families are nearby, as is my church. Music and books surround me; my computer is my constant companion.

Through all the highs and lows, I have maintained my focus over the past five years and achieved important goals: conducting research for my doctoral thesis; completing the eighty-four page thesis, *The Dynamics of Emotion in the Personal Christian Experience*; receiving my Doctor of Theology Degree; and the writing of this memoir. Now I am contemplating ideas for a science fiction allegory of the origin of the universe and man, himself.

May your higher power bless you and keep you;
May the force of the universe and beyond shine its face on you,
And give you peace of soul and spirit,
This day and forevermore.
May a song find its way to your heart.